Small
House
Living
Australia

Smart design in homes
of 90m² or less

Tom.
How to squeeze
a quart into
a pint pot.
CF

Small House Living Australia

VIKING
an imprint of
PENGUIN BOOKS

Catherine Foster

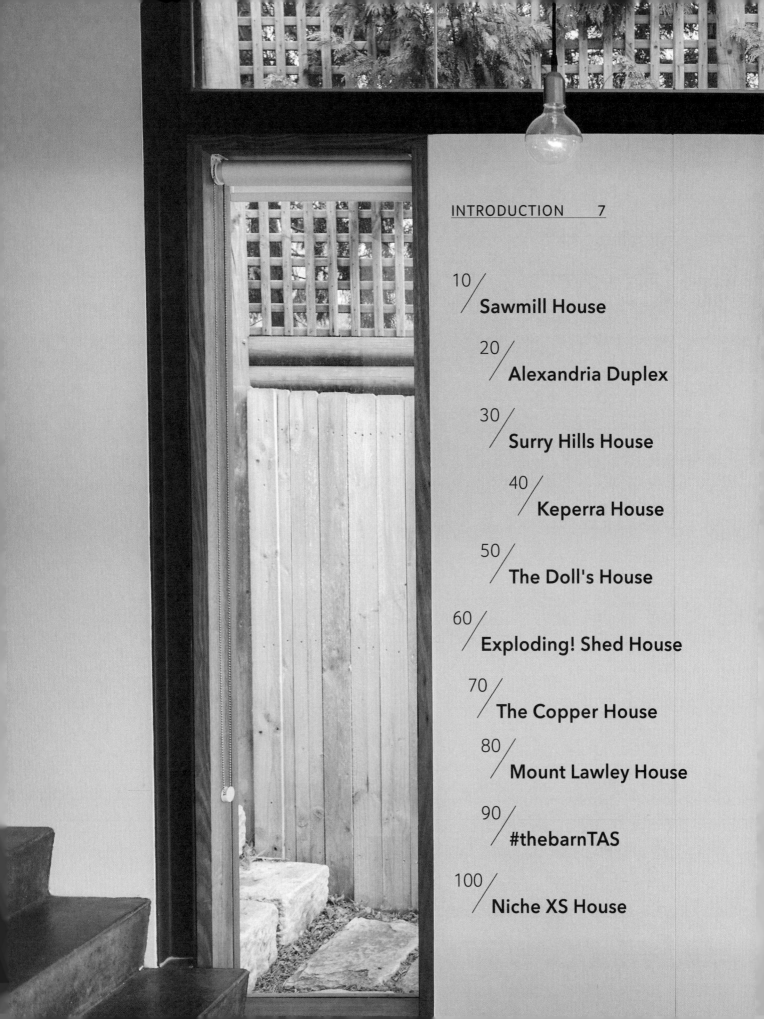

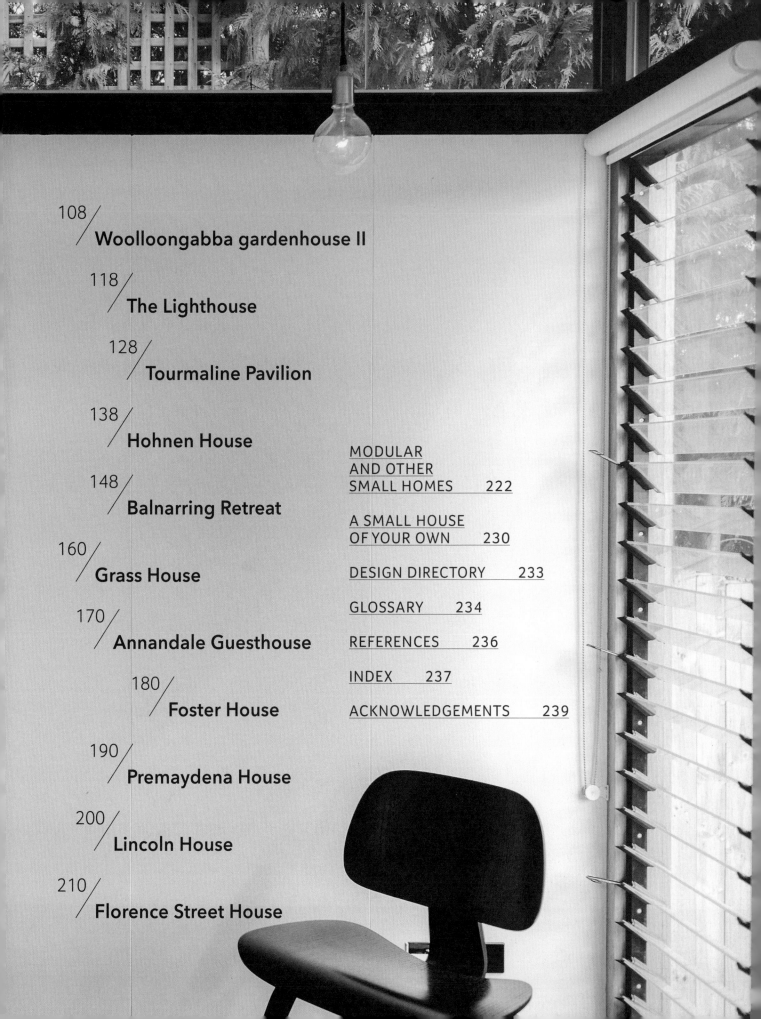

INTRODUCTION

Australia is famous – perhaps infamous – for building some of the biggest new homes in the world. The average footprint of new builds in Australia hovers around 231m² – less than the mammoth dimensions of newly-built houses in the United States, to be sure, but 30 per cent larger than what they were thirty years ago. New Zealand and Canada are not far behind.

The relentless upward march of home sizes comes with significant environmental and social costs, not least the burden it throws on first time buyers seeking to gain a foothold in the property market. Happily, more and more Australians are recognising that size is not everything. This book celebrates this return to more modest dimensions. The examples in these pages, none of which exceed 90m², demonstrates that with careful attention to design and a bit of clever thinking, a reduction in size does not require compromises in quality or sophistication.

The reasons for this trend are not clear. Generation Y and Millennials have been priced out of traditional homes and that has without doubt contributed to a greater willingness to accept smaller dwellings. But it does not account for cashed-up baby boomers choosing to downsize radically when selecting their retirement accommodation, or explain the kind of building those same baby boomers are commissioning - tiny, design-dense gems full of architectural wit and charm.

It seems there has been a growing sea-change in our housing philosophies – a developing sense that a home's worth is not commensurate with its size, or perhaps even that living modestly is preferable to opulent expense. Whatever the reasons may be, the results in architectural terms are splendid.

In cities, the changing attitudes find expression in many forms. Whether witty insertions on tiny infill sites, secondary dwellings in suburban backyards, innovative renovations of nineteenth century houses, each has its place in the ever increasing diversity of the urban landscape.

An example of an inner-city addition is David Luck's Grass House in Fitzroy, Victoria (page 160). Moody as a teenager, it shakes a grassy head on a tight Melbourne corner, exemplifying how issues of permeability and site coverage can be overcome when clever architecture marries a planning process that encourages, rather than thwarts, innovation.

PAGE 1
Inexpensive hoop pine plywood is as useful as a robust and attractive interior lining as it is in more traditional uses.

PAGE 2
Wrapping two planes of the stairwell with one large window fills the interior with light and is an eye-catching feature when viewed from the exterior.

CONTENTS PAGE
Contemporary louvre windows allow ventilation without compromising security.

OPPOSITE
Work space functionality is represented through the choice of materials used – plywood and polished concrete.

8

The relationship between planners and architects was often less harmonious in the recent past. Only a decade earlier, David Langston-Jones went all the way to the NSW Land and Environment Court for the right to build two units of residential accommodation on a 150m² site deemed 'uninhabitable' because of its size and semi-commercial location. Today his Alexandria Duplex (page 20) is a clear example of how a compact inner city site can provide accommodation that is elegant and comfortable.

In the suburbs, the trend towards smaller housing manifests in the proliferation of secondary dwellings. Studios, granny flats, garden houses, guesthouses, pods or pads – call them what you will – these small self-contained homes are increasingly popular in suburban backyards, due in large part to the recent changes in town planning regulations which, in some states, encourage the construction of these kind of ancillary homes.

Emma Hohnen's self-built gem (page 138) is a case in point. A simple structure constructed largely of recycled materials and readymade components, it is home to Hohnen and her children, and allows the main house on the site to be let out. The Tourmaline Pavilion (page 128) is another backyard addition that houses a mother and her children, albeit one that originated in the studio of award winning architect Peter Stutchbury. A-CH's award-winning Keperra House (page 40) is a 45m² lock-up-and-leave bolthole for a baby-booming traveller.

Another emerging trend sees owners combining residential and commercial space in ways not seen since the nineteenth century. David Weir's Exploding! Shed (page 60) houses an illustrator and her studio-workshop while Robeson Architects' Mount Lawley House (page 80) is both live-work space for the architect herself, and a clever use of a site so awkward it was once considered unusable.

Renovations of existing housing also has its place. Studio Edwards' Doll's House (page 50) and Ben Giles' Surry Hills House (page 30) are very different examples of how these once less than perfect nineteenth century dwellings are compromised no longer. They may be small – indeed tiny – but they are light-filled and stylishly aspirational.

The trend to smaller housing has even found its way to the countryside, where the costs and constraints of city living do not apply. Instead, there is a growing desire to live lightly on the land and to harmonise with, rather than intrude upon, the pastoral idyll of rural Australia.

Archier's Sawmill House (page 10) is not exactly a live-work space but is rather a home that shares a working site. The name is a giveaway, although the sawmill for which the site is named is long defunct. Instead the owner, a sculptor, has the luxury of space. Buildings that once housed the sawmill are his workshops, while his home is separated from the noise and dust a short distance away. Budget, not block size, was the main constraint and the home is not large. Nevertheless, the small space is made generous by verandas enclosed within moveable screens and retracting roofs, with hints of bright landscapes glimpsed from sheltered interiors.

Holiday homes have different needs to full time residences. As they are rarely intended as permanent accommodation, a harmonious interaction with their surroundings can be prioritised. Cooking, bathing and sleeping arrangements must function effortlessly, whether accommodation for large numbers or a few is required, and security while uninhabited cannot be overlooked. Among the examples in these pages, interwoven yet proud in their landscapes, are Allison Hopper's Foster House (page 180), Branch Studio's Balnarring Retreat (page 148) and Micho + Associates Premaydena House (page 190) – small dream 'homes away from home'.

Though each one is unique, the projects in this book prove that we do not need to give into the cult of size to live well. Clever application of the fundamentals of good design, together with efficient use of materials and space, means small size need be no barrier to architectural magic. Building smaller also offers solutions in a world where grappling with questions of cost and sustainability is ever more relevant.

Sawmill House

88M² + 42M² VERANDA

Yackandandah, VIC

Archier

Photography by
Benjamin Hosking

Awards

Australian Institute of
Architects 2015 National
Architecture Awards:
National Award for Regional
Architecture – Houses (New)

Houses Awards 2015:
New House Under 200m²

In the deep, hot silence of the Victorian countryside lies a small
family home, innovative not only in design terms, but also as an
example of how a collaborative local regulatory environment
permitted architect Chris Gilbert and his client, brother and
sculptor Ben Gilbert, to make use of their combined skill set to
build Ben and his young family a home. This in itself might not
seem extraordinary but the simplified design and documentation
stage, that allowed for experimental problem-solving while the
build was in progress, is an almost unknown luxury in the highly-
regulated building approval process in Australian cities.

Unusual too was both the architect and client's wish to make
constructive use of locally-sourced building waste product. This was
not mere cost expediency. With a site that had once housed both
goldmine and sawmill, and was still in use as the client's workshop
and studio, they saw the inclusion of materials that referenced
this industrial heritage as being integral to the project. 'Being part
of a narrative – where the price had already been paid – was an
important concept to us,' is how Gilbert explained the construction
of perimeter walls from 207 one-tonne blocks of waste concrete.
'Each was made with a different endeavour in mind - a bridge, a
footpath, a home, and each have different layers of colour and
texture. In a way, they echo the sedimentary layers exposed from
the workings of the goldmine'.

PREVIOUS PAGE
A combination of folding and
sliding screens allow the deck
to function virtually year-round
as a sheltered extension to the
living space.

OPPOSITE
A material palette of red
stringybark and exposed concrete
contrasts with the tactile warmth
of the bed and lawn beyond. When
fully open, the pivoting door swings
out of sight so that the interior
and exterior appear to be one
continuous space.

Red stringybark glows on the walls and ceiling, and brass-lined storage alcoves glint like little jewel boxes

The monumental nature of these outsize building blocks could be the dominating element of the design. Certainly, they confer a presence that cannot be denied, but it is their eloquent contrast with the delicacy of the second – the slatted, rough-sawn macrocarpa screens that clad much of the front elevation – that causes the sum of the parts to become more than merely unusual. Here, where a retractable roof and oversize sliding and folding screens shelter and, when necessary, enclose the veranda – notions of light and dark, transience and permanence are playfully explored in a language that owes as much to that of the woolshed as it does Modernist simplicity.

Because the veranda operates as year-round living space, the enclosed dwelling to its rear measures no more than 88m², a cost-effective use of both budget and resources. Sheltered by the veranda and its moveable screens, this core needed only light containment. An oversized glazed sliding wall, which retracts to allow both spaces to operate as one large informal living, socialising and eating area, fulfils this function. The complexity of installing such a large piece of moveable glazing required the input of another family member, Chris and Ben's father, retired telecommunications engineer and (in Chris's words) 'supreme tinkerer', Ray Gilbert.

The lightweight nature of both these inner and outer northerly elements, which can open simultaneously to embrace the view across the water-filled quarry, is counterbalanced by a south-facing rear largely recessed into a sheltering hillside. Windows here are necessarily small and high-level. The sole bedroom on the other hand, is dramatically exposed. East-facing, and with the whole outer facade taking the form of a glazed pivoting door, it opens onto a small, grassy courtyard, sheltered and secure in the lee of a right-angled continuation of the concrete block perimeter wall.

The living space is heated by a substantial wood burner, but the sense of warmth is not purely physical. Red stringybark glows on the walls and ceiling, and brass-lined storage alcoves glint like little jewel boxes in the deepest, most private recesses – the impression is almost womblike.

TOP
When closed, the sliding screens shelter the outdoor living area while still allowing light and outlook through the slats.

BOTTOM
The small grassy garden that leads from the bedroom is deeply sheltered on two sides by the concrete block wall. On the third it connects to the veranda and the enclosed space behind itD. Services are concealed behind a slatted timber wall on the southern side.

Although not milled on site, both the macrocarpa and the red stringybark are local. So too was the way of working that made the onsite evolution of the design and building possible. 'We had an immensely helpful and understanding building surveyor, and we could tap into a hugely collaborative and skilled local work force. There was no sense of competition. It was all about getting it done.'

Overall the structure in some ways defies convention but does not try to reinvent the wheel. What it did without a doubt, was in Chris Gilbert's words, to construct that most precious structure of all, 'a bridge between brothers'.

OPPOSITE, TOP
The entrance is via a slatted metal bridge.

BOTTOM
Solar energy provides year-round electricity, while water collected off the roof is stored in tanks buried underground in the raised area to the rear.

OVER PAGE
Red stringybark lines the kitchen alcove, contrasting both visually and texturally with the brass cladding of the cupboard doors.

Design Notes

/ Repurposing locally available waste material made a major design statement and simultaneously benefitted both the environment and the budget.

/ Enclosing the veranda with moveable screens expanded the living space inexpensively.

/ With many of the walls and the roof of the veranda being moveable, weather and outlook are controllable throughout the year.

Sawmill House

<u>88M² + 42M² VERANDA</u>
Yackandandah, VIC
Archier

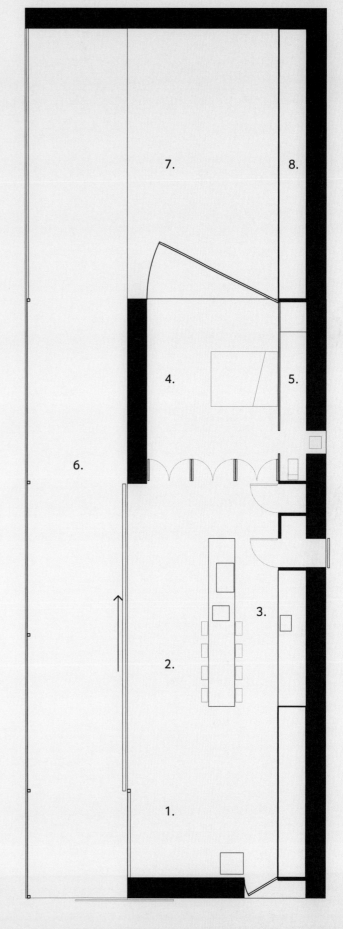

1   Lounge
2   Dining
3   Kitchen
4   Bedroom
5   Bathroom
6   Deck
7   Courtyard
8   Services

Alexandria Duplex

68M² + GARAGE

Alexandria, Sydney, NSW

David Langston-Jones

Photography by
Michael Nicholson

Awards

Australian Institute of
Architects 2008 NSW
Architecture Awards:
Commendation for
Residential Architecture –
Multiple Housing

Pioneers never have it easy, and architects designing outside the norm seldom do either. Refuting a decision from South Sydney Council that the subdivision into two small lots would lead to 'uninhabitable' dwellings was at the extreme end of difficulty. Bloodied but unbowed, co-owner and architect David Langston-Jones took the fight all the way to a two-day hearing at the NSW Land and Environment Court. His victory continues to influence the planning laws of NSW to this day.

Coming from London, where building on difficult brown field sites was unusual but not unheard of, Langston-Jones knew that although the 151m² Alexandria site was tight, and in a location that in 1999–2002 was more commercial than residential, it was eminently suitable for the small-scale development he had in mind. 'The decisions that drove my partner and me to want our home here were personal and spontaneous, but I knew from my work in London that sites like this were very usable. I also knew that designing in a way that was suitable for a twenty-first century lifestyle would not sacrifice comfortable living spaces or aesthetic responses.'

The result was worth fighting for. Running along the rear of four Victorian terraced houses, the block consequently has a long frontage, and it was embracing this aspect that allowed Langston-Jones to insert two small homes – each mirroring the other along a central axis. With a material palette of grey painted corrugated Zincalume and stacked concrete block acknowledging the once highly industrial character of the neighbourhood, the facade it presents to the world is hardly cosy. Austerity is however leavened by the rhythms set up by recessing the entry point and balconies, and by using a finer gauge corrugation to clad them, thus producing the impression they are larger and deeper than they are.

PREVIOUS PAGE
An austere exterior material palette of grey Zincalume and stacked concrete block were a deliberate choice to reflect, and comment upon, the industrial roots of the location.

OPPOSITE
Warm timber tones, fine gauged Zincalume and pops of primary colour contrasting with curved and angular forms make for an intriguing interior.

Similar tricks with perspective were used to visually expand the footprint of each dwelling. As Langston-Jones explains, 'With small spaces like these you have to employ all sorts of devices to enhance the impression of size. Mirrors, the placement of glazing to allow the windows to be uncluttered by coverings and yet not compromise privacy, opposing light sources so light penetrates at all times of the day – all of these help create the illusion that the floorplan is bigger than it is.'

The positioning of the staircase was also vital. Wrapping around the rear of the kitchen and into the part of the garage where the bonnet of a car would be, the space usually wasted by the positioning of a stairwell within a room actually becomes a design element of its own. Constructed, like all the internal joinery, from American walnut, it invites a subtle engagement with the private world of the sleeping area on the mezzanine above.

Enclosed under the mezzanine, the living area and its accompanying kitchen is not huge, but using the same flooring material to connect the interior and exterior spaces enhances the impression of spaciousness. So too does the expansive double height void of the adjacent dining area, and the large areas of glazing in the wall beyond. Composed of a combination of sliding doors, louvres set at 45° angles and clerestory windows above, the multiple openings on this facade allow the house to remain ventilated and well-lit no matter what the time of day or year.

The visual warmth of walnut for joinery and cabinetry in the interior serves as a metaphor for the warmth of a domestic life. This is an impression its architect is willing to acknowledge. 'This was always conceived as a home for myself and my partner, and everything in it reflects that to some extent.' The splashes of primary colour – red on the splashback, yellow on the Le Corbusier *Grand Confort* sofa, green on the concealed speakers – along with the careful consideration of the size and style of key furnishings serve the same purpose. 'We chose the furniture specifically for the home. The armchair acts as a kind of baseball glove, catching the space and confining it – we had the armrest custom made for the sofa in American walnut to tie in with other aspects of the joinery. Even the freestanding green column is treated like a piece of furniture.'

OPPOSITE, TOP LEFT AND RIGHT
A large dining area located in the double height atrium beside the courtyard garden is fully glazed along its exterior wall. Further lit by light entering through the clerestory windows on the opposing wall, this area is as imposing as it is practical.

BOTTOM
Bright colour accents and recessed lighting make the interior complex and interesting.

26

With small spaces like these you have to employ all kinds of devices to enhance the impression of size

OPPOSITE, TOP LEFT

A Japanese inspired slatted timber floor in the shower area contrasts with the functionality of tiles and a Zincalume ceiling in the adjacent bathroom

OPPOSITE, TOP RIGHT
AND BOTTOM

With no need for covered parking, the owner has converted the garage into an office. The space beneath the ascending staircase is used for storing small scale items, while larger objects are kept out of sight in the purpose-built unit on the opposite wall.

OVER PAGE

The dining area and courtyard are interconnected by a wall of glazing. Because the same flooring material is used in both the interior and exterior, the impression of size is enhanced.

Ten years on from completion, Langston-Jones judges what he fought so hard for as successful on every level. 'I am very happy with how it functions. It shows that when we put our minds to it, we can live in cities as densely as they do in the old world, but in ways that work well for how we live in the twenty-first century.'

Design Notes

/ The east-facing shared courtyard garden visually and physically extends both dwellings.

/ Furniture was chosen with care to respect the interior scale, and mirrors, plus the careful placement of glazing, were used to make the spaces appear bigger than they are.

/ Glazing the double-height void above the dining area, and the wall onto the courtyard, enhances the impression of space without compromising privacy.

Alexandria Duplex

<u>68M² + GARAGE</u>
Alexandria, Sydney, NSW
David Langston-Jones Architect

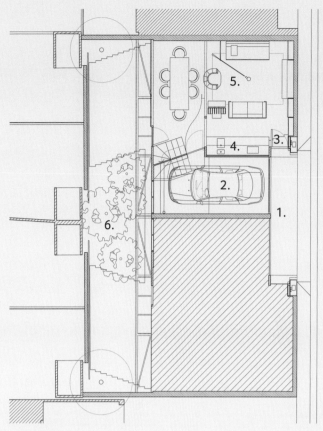

Ground floor

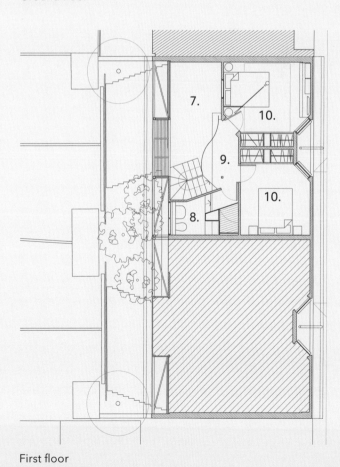

1   Shared porch

2   Garage

3   Entry

4   Kitchen

5   Living area

6   Shared courtyard garden

7   Void

8   Bathroom

9   Landing

10   Bedroom

First floor

Surry Hills House

<u>82M²</u>

Surry Hills, Sydney, NSW

Ben Giles Architect

Photography by
Katherine Lu

Intensification, densification – both are buzz words in twenty-first century urban planning. Call it what you will, it is a reality for city dwellers across Australia. The reasons are many, but chief amongst them is the growing appreciation that environmental resources are limited, land is expensive and that one- and two-person households are increasingly common. Somewhat counterintuitively, however, intensification is not an exclusively modern development – the heritage areas in Australia's largest cities have been closely built since the earliest days of colonial settlement.

Belinda Tee's terrace home is a case in point. Almost 150 years old, it was built to fully occupy its 68m² wedge-shaped site. The modest two-storey terrace cottage drops away at street level in an agglomeration of scrappily-built additions, almost to the rear boundary. With a street frontage of 3.85m narrowing to only 2m at the rear, the spaces were awkward, and light and outlook minimal.

Bringing the site, as much as the dwelling upon it, into the twenty-first century was a challenge which fell to architect Ben Giles. Fortunately he relishes making a small space work. 'It's largely about getting light in, and here we had the ideal orientation – the rear faces north – but the existing additions blocked light as well as just being dysfunctional. The site is tight but allowing light to penetrate right into the core of the structure enhances what space there is. Demolishing the additions and stripping the original structure back to its dirt sub-floor and dusty brick walls was the only way forward.'

Located in a heritage conservation zone, neither the street frontage could be altered, nor could any additions be visible from the opposite side of the street. However, once sightlines had been established, maximising height and volume was nonetheless permissible. Because the original roofline was steeply pitched, a double height extension towards the rear of the site could be installed while remaining unseen from the front. As a terrace, it was also possible to build to the side boundaries. Even so, allowing for a small suntrap rear garden, the internal dimensions over two levels amounted to just over 80m².

PREVIOUS PAGE.
The atrium at the core of this narrow terrace has transformed the interior by allowing light to reach deep into the rooms on either side of it. Mechanised louvres allow it to act as a thermal chimney ventilating the building in summer and encouraging warmth to circulate during winter.

OPPOSITE
Adding a living area to the rear of the atrium with a bedroom above has completely transformed the usability of the house as a whole.

34

No longer a dark Victorian cubby, the structure which now graces this narrow backstreet is an inspirational contemporary home

Although much improved from the original minuscule footprint, 80m² is still not huge, and Giles' reorganisation of the interior is a masterpiece of maximising space. To achieve the desired outcome, it was necessary that every room in the house, save the bedroom on the upper level, be substantially reworked. Even the front door was not spared. With a mere 3.4m internal width, hallways were an unnecessary luxury, and removing the wall between what would once have been a tiny Victorian parlour and the entrance hall was essential. The space now functions as a small and welcoming dining room-cum-workspace that somehow feels both Victorian and contemporary at the same time.

Circulation remains tight but relocating the stairway into the very centre of the building allowed one side of the galley kitchen to tuck beneath it, with enough room alongside to act as a passageway to the new extension at the rear. Situating the bathroom directly above the kitchen minimised plumbing costs and also allowed both rooms to benefit from the 'borrowed' light and outlook that filters through the gaps created by the angles of the staircase. These have been left unglazed, partly for ventilation and partly as a quirky design detail.

So far, so straightforward. But as Giles points out, light in a small space is everything, and it is here that the Victorian cottage leaves its past behind and opens its arms to the twenty-first century. The result is quite literally astonishing – where once a low-ceilinged kitchen lean-to would have blocked light and outlook, there now stands a crisply detailed double-height glazed atrium. This not only imparts a sense of verticality, but it also imbues the modest dimensions of the interior with an unexpected sense of grandeur. Through it, light flows to illuminate both the more intimate original cottage to the front and the sunny openness of the new rear extension.

The perfect place to stargaze on a cloudless night, this light-filled core is as functional as it is visually dramatic. Heat-minimising E-glazing and a line of mechanised louvres mounted just below the skylight allow it to act as a thermal chimney, ventilating and purging this deep, narrow building of excess heat in summer, while encouraging warmth to circulate in winter.

OPPOSITE, TOP LEFT
One side of the galley kitchen slots in under the staircase which, in a departure from the norm in terrace houses, is located centrally rather than along an outer wall. This allows for a passageway between the front and rear of the building to run along its outer edge.

TOP RIGHT
The light-filled atrium that is the eye-catching core of the building also has a practical function.

BOTTOM
The front entrance opens directly into what would have been the parlour of the Victorian house. With an internal width of 3.4m there was no room for a passageway, and the wall that once separated it from the entrance hallway was removed.

On the ground floor, the extension beyond contains a small, pleasantly proportioned living room with floor-to-ceiling bi-folds connecting directly to a bijou garden at its rear. On the level above is the master bedroom. This quiet haven of adult sophistication is lightly connected to the front of the house by its own high level bridge. A small rear balcony visually and practically extends the footprint, and serves as a privacy buffer and shade barrier for the living area below.

No longer a dark Victorian cubby, the structure which now graces this narrow backstreet is an inspirational contemporary home – one that complements rather than contradicts its origins. It isn't huge but every millimetre is functional and beautiful. What more can a small, twenty-first century family want?

Design Notes

/ The glazed ceiling of the centrally-located atrium floods the interior with light, and rooms with no exterior walls – the kitchen and bathroom – borrow from this light source through unglazed geometrically shaped openings.

/ The small rear balcony from the master bedroom provides privacy for the living room below as well as sun protection from the north.

/ Full height, wall-to-wall, bi-fold doors connect the living room to the small rear garden, allowing the two to operate as one large open space.

OPPOSITE, TOP LEFT
A skylight made from heat minimising E-glass and temperature-activated mechanised louvres control overheating while flooding the interior with light.

TOP RIGHT
One side of the galley kitchen is recessed into a wall of storage that eliminates visual clutter.

BOTTOM
Bi-fold doors connect the living room with the north-facing patio to the rear. Light entering from this direction, plus that from the atrium, visually expands the modest dimensions.

OVER PAGE
Being in a conservation area, the street frontage is unchanged. Only crisp new render gives any indication to the scale of works that was required to bring this cottage into the 21st century.

Surry Hills House

<u>82M²</u>
Surry Hills, Sydney, NSW
Ben Giles Architect

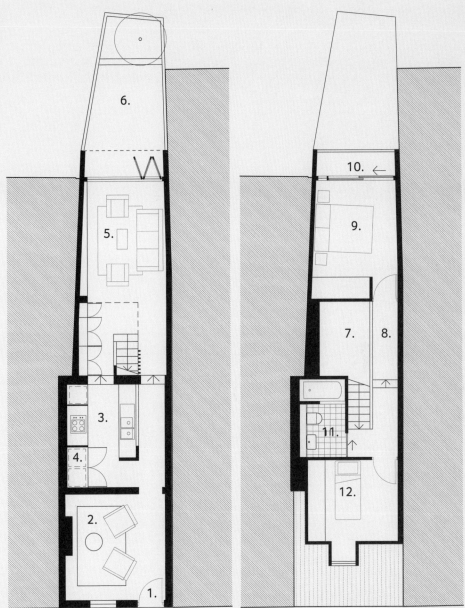

Ground floor   First floor

<u>1</u>   Entry
<u>2</u>   Sitting
<u>3</u>   Kitchen
<u>4</u>   Laundry
<u>5</u>   Living
<u>6</u>   Courtyard
<u>7</u>   Void
<u>8</u>   Bridge
<u>9</u>   Bedroom 1
<u>10</u>   Balcony
<u>11</u>   Bathroom
<u>12</u>   Bedroom 2

Keperra House

45M²

Keperra, Queensland

A–CH (Atelier Chen Hung)

Photography by
Alicia Taylor

Award

43

Australian Institute
of Architects 2013 National
Architecture Awards: National
Award for Small Project
Architecture

In Australia's super-size-me society, downsizing in real estate is all too often confused with downgrading. Small houses as clever as A-CH's Keperra House refute that notion thoroughly.

Built to leverage the client's existing home to allow a comfortable lifestyle with opportunities for travel, the architects took advantage of local planning regulations that allow owners to construct small secondary dwellings (up to 80m²) to be built on suburban plots without going through the full consent process. With a mature jacaranda and a slightly elevated position above a luxuriant creek reserve, the site was ideal.

Owner Michael Alroe had no wish to build to the full 80m² allowed. Rather, he sought a small, easy-care, lock-up-and-leave home, robust in construction, and of an architectural merit that reflected his lifelong interest in contemporary architecture. 'I could see from their website these architects were young and innovative, and since they were a small practice I really benefited from their enthusiasm and attention to detail.'

At a mere 45m² Alroe's home demonstrates how small can indeed be clever, practically as well as aesthetically. As architect James Hung comments, the starting point was not to slavishly reference the vernacular architecture of the area. 'We had no preconceived ideas about a particular type of building. Both Melody (Chen) and I like to use materials that have a depth and texture to them – that work with the landscape – but in ways that aren't necessarily the first that come to mind.'

PREVIOUS PAGE
Galvanised sheet iron and poured concrete are an unusual combination of materials in suburban surroundings where timber bungalows are the norm.

OPPOSITE
Sliding doors and shutters on both sides of the pavilion-like central section of the structure allow cooling, shelter and outlook in summer, yet close easily to provide the lock-up-and-leave security the owner required.

44

It's not that the materials are unusual, it's the pairing of them with the building type and the location that surprises

Thus, in a suburb of mid-century timber bungalows, they took inspiration from the agricultural buildings of the same era and by using their galvanised iron and concrete material palette produced a structure of such striking appearance that strangers knock on the door wanting to know more. As Hung explains, 'It's not that the materials are unusual, it's the pairing of them with the building type and the location that surprises.'

Perched on a steep embankment near the rear of the site, the elongated nature of the structure operates as what its architects describe as an 'inhabited wall' between the lush wilderness that is the creek reserve and the domesticity of the suburban garden. Large sections of the wall and the recessed footings, which encourage the impression that the structure floats above its surroundings, are constructed from poured concrete. Horizontal patterns of the timber formwork impressed on their surfaces obliquely reference the neighbouring weatherboard constructions. Upper walls, and the sliding doors and shutters that allow the building to be fully secured when needed, are clad in silvery sheets of galvanised steel - a luxurious repurposing of this most utilitarian of building materials.

In form too, Hung and Chen rework simple themes and in ways that maximised the budget. Lopping asymmetric chunks from either end of the structure and inserting a central, lightly-built pavilion between the two more solidly built pods that form the outer structures, transforms what could be no more than a simple progression of three narrow rooms into something altogether more intriguing. The architects see a further benefit. 'These three zones direct the views in different ways, with the living room having the most liberated view across the reserve, the deck intermediate because it faces in both directions, and the bedroom is, of course, more intimate.'

The use of robust materials more familiar in industrial settings continues inside. While the honeyed gold of hoop pine plywood is the dominant colour, black Formply – a specialist plywood used for concrete formwork – enlivens the recesses and cupboard interiors. Both materials are durable and inexpensive. Living and cooking functions are contained in one pod and sleeping and bathing in another, with the 'tent-like' structure of the central core coming into its own in the dog-days of summer. When both sides are opened to the breeze, it is the closest thing to living comfortably under canvas as can be imagined.

A granny flat, a secondary dwelling or a minor home? Each are different names for what in this case is an elegantly downscaled dwelling. Open for everyday living, or packed down for travel, here is a home that oozes design excellence from every pore.

Design Notes

/ Simple materials, used in unexpected ways, are both budget-friendly and eyecatching.

/ Insulated pods slung on either side of a transparent living core are a climate friendly and cost-effective way of stretching the budget.

/ Positioning at the rear of the site benefits both the original dwelling and the new, with privacy, views and outdoor space available for both.

OPPOSITE, TOP
The asymmetric shape of the kitchen does not detract from its functionality, yet it was an inexpensive way to add interest and complexity to the form of the building itself.

BOTTOM
Both sides of the central pavilion open to allow as much ventilation, shade and outlook as required, while a full-height glazed sliding door connects the kitchen to the surrounding garden.

OVER PAGE
A dramatic exterior form gives the impression that this is as much installation as habitation.

Keperra House

45M²
Keperra, Queensland
A-CH (Atelier Chen Hung)

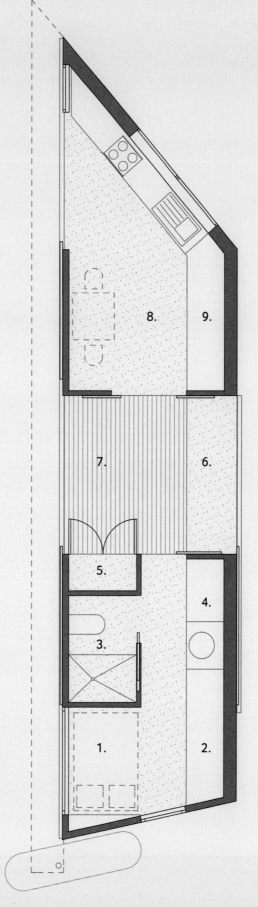

1   Bedroom
2   Robe
3   Bathroom
4   Laundry
5   Store
6   Entry
7   Deck
8   Living/Kitchen
9   Seat

The Doll's House

70M²

Fitzroy, Melbourne, VIC

Studio Edwards

Photography by
Fraser Marsden

Deep narrow sites with laneways to the rear were the city plan of choice for nineteenth-century urban planners in Australia as they allowed a cost-effective solution for sewage and rubbish disposal. Unlike the crowded cities of the old world however, land in Australia was comparatively plentiful. Working class suburbs could remain low level, with narrow houses placed close to the street frontage extending back into deep, narrow sites. For a settler society unused to the Australian sun, the consequent lack of light was a bonus.

But the needs of twenty-first century Fitzroy are a far cry from those which shaped its urban plan. Ben Edwards' client was typical of the newcomers. 'The client wanted the location – its proximity to the CBD and the local amenities. It didn't matter that this was the smallest house in the street. It came with the typical linear site so making use of this was the obvious way to address the lack of light while adding to the footprint.'

The new larger footprint is still merely 70m², but retaining the street frontage and structure of the original cottage while separating it from its utilitarian rear has allowed light and an intimate connection with the revealed outdoor spaces, where previously there was none. All internal walls in the original structure were demolished, so that what was once a minuscule dwelling now functions as a well-proportioned living space. With the entrance straight off the street, and no hallways or internal doors to clutter or obstruct, it feels surprisingly spacious. The original loft above – accessible only by a ladder to avoid the need for a space-guzzling staircase – has been retained as occasional guest accommodation.

PREVIOUS PAGE
The kitchen in one of two new additions links the original cottage at the front to the new bedroom at the rear.

OPPOSITE
The horizontal boards across the floor in what is now the living area give an indication of the size of the two rooms that formed the original cottage. Partially exposed brick walls and inexpensive plywood shelving are both a design statement and an acknowledgment of the historical roots of the neighbourhood.

Two new additions placed along the full length of the long southern boundary make full use of the depth of the site. The rearmost of these is a generous bedroom, while the innermost, connected to both front and rear structures by a pair of truncated passages, contains the kitchen and dining area.

Both walls of this central core are fully glazed oblique angles allowing ample room for the two resultant courtyards to act as what Edwards describes as 'lungs' to ventilate and light the spaces on either side. The outer wall of the rear of these courtyards is also glazed and the additional light through the central kitchen and dining area makes the house appear larger than it in fact is. When budget permits, the rear wall to the original structure will also be opened up and glazed, allowing uninterrupted sightlines through the full depth of the site.

While such deft manipulations enhance the impression of spaciousness, so too do the raw interior finishes in the original part of the building, where partially exposed brick walls contrast with simple plywood shelving and café style wiring. In contrast, the new areas are distinctly Scandi-modern, with white paint and clean lines.

These could be viewed as a fashion statement, given this is a location where industrial grunge has almost become an artform in its own right. Edwards' version is rather more than that. Instead it is a design ethos that celebrates imperfection, while acknowledging the historical roots of the neighbourhood. It also has the advantage of making best use of a tight budget. 'Raw and untreated finishes are obviously a cost-effective way of completing interiors – this is a prime example of architecture on a budget – but used like they have been here, and by leaving the arrangement of the previous spaces apparent, they retain the memory of what's gone before.'

And while broken plaster and exposed wiring acknowledge the historical context, small areas of beaten brass and gold Alucobond playfully lend a contemporary touch of luxe. These elements focus attention onto how the site as a whole has been repurposed for contemporary use. They also work overtime to bounce light into the deepest corners - even into the shadowy depths of the front room.

A small change of level, and a change from recycled timber flooring to polished concrete between the old and new, further emphasises how the historical importance of the original structure has been allowed to inform, but not dominate, the narrative of the building itself.

TOP LEFT
Outlook to the bedroom is provided by one of the two gravelled courtyards.

TOP RIGHT
Both this courtyard, and the one between the kitchen and the living room, act as 'lungs' to the building – ventilating and lighting it in ways not conceived of in the original Victorian structure

BOTTOM RIGHT
The asymmetry of the purpose-built kitchen table echoes, but does not replicate, that of the central addition that houses the kitchen.

BOTTOM LEFT
A change in level between the rear addition and the kitchen adds interest to the simple rectilinear structure.

The client wanted the location – its proximity to the CBD and local amenties. It didn't matter that this was the smallest house in the street

OPPOSITE, TOP

The addition of a beaten brass splash-back to the simple slot kitchen is a playful touch of contemporary luxe. Using interesting but slightly more expensive materials sparingly stretches the budget and playfully alludes to how once purely utilitarian dwellings have been repurposed for contemporary use.

BOTTOM

A ladder takes the place of a staircase to the loft (which doubles as both occasional guest accommodation and storage). The original fireplace alongside the line of exposed brick indicates where this area was once two rooms.

OVER PAGE

No wider than a car is long, the modest dimensions of houses of this sort were once the norm for this suburb.

In terms of floor space, this is still a modest home. But while it was once dark and woefully uninterested in the possibilities of its site, it now serves as a clever reminder that the basic principles of good architecture can rescue even the most problematic of dwellings. Edwards, by allowing light and flow to interact with volume and aesthetic pleasure, has enabled twenty-first century living to intermarry with nineteenth-century pragmatism. The result is quirky, clever and altogether beguiling.

Design Notes

/ Two courtyards inserted between the three living zones light and ventilate the interiors spaces to each side of them.

/ Setting the glazed doors which access the courtyards on angles allows the deep, narrow site to appear wider than it is.

/ Internal finishes in the original part of the structure are deliberately left seemingly unfinished to reflect both the historical context and the owner's contemporary desire for an uncomplicated way of life.

The Doll's House

70M²
Fitzroy, Melbourne, VIC
Studio Edwards

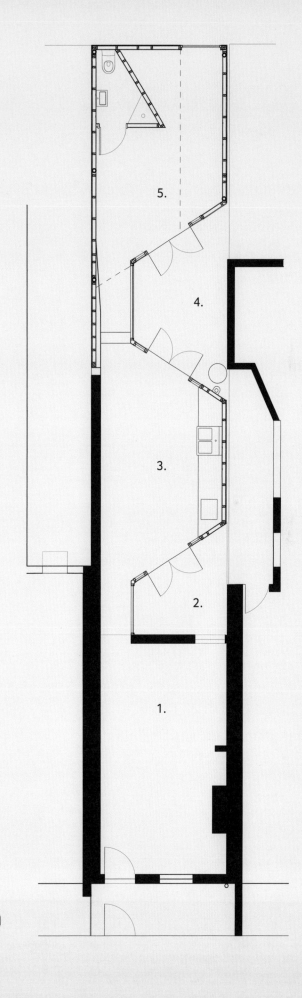

1____Living
2____Garden
3____Kitchen/Dining
4____Garden
5____Bedroom

Exploding! Shed House

60M² ACCOMMODATION + 30M² WORKSPACE

Mount Lawley, Perth, WA

David Weir Architects

Photography by
Dion Robeson

A designer and illustrator who 'gets messy' when she works, Karen Hearn is not an architect's typical client. Then again, the Mount Lawley home and attached workplace is far from characteristic of Mount Lawley. Unlike the surrounding suburb, with its typical mid-century weatherboard bungalows and cottages, architect David Weir designed a structure as much of its moment as its owner.

Although comparatively straightforward, the brief carried the weight of high client expectations, and Weir was aware that the outcome was never expected to be conventional. 'The client was chasing a small house, something that was easy to take care of, something that could be done to a budget. A house with a yard and a studio workshop - something that would be beautiful and comfortable, and that could be lived in for a long time.'

The fact that Hearn expects to live in her home indefinitely was crucial. The goal was not to protect an investment – instead, the structure could be designed entirely to fulfil the needs and wishes of the client. The site did not need to be 'optimised'. Retaining a usable part of the yard and protecting the beauty of its mature jacaranda was more important.

There is only one bedroom, and even that is only separated from the living area by a linen curtain. Light enters from all directions, and large glazed doors and windows to the front and rear visually expand the compact interiors still further. Where rooms are overlooked from the adjacent laneway, slot windows located at floor level allow light to wash across the polished concrete floor without compromising privacy.

Abbreviated walls and furniture are the only elements that define the spaces, although the elevation of the living area on a low plinth produces an unexpected note of drama. Pragmatism rather than pure aesthetics drove this particular decision. The roots of the precious jacaranda, too delicate to be built on, had to be protected, and raising the floor was one of many strategies employed during the build to protect it. Weir was happy to accommodate it. 'We lifted the floor, hand-dug trenches and wrapped the trunk to disturb it as little as possible. Trees like this bring so much life to the site, they must be protected at all costs.'

PREVIOUS PAGE
The floor of the living area was raised to accommodate the fragile roots of a large jacaranda that shelters and beautifies the site. Glazed walls allow light to reach the deepest interior spaces.

OPPOSITE
Polished concrete floors act as a solar sink to assist in heat storage in the cooler months while respecting the workman-like aesthetic of this live-work space.

The roots of the precious jacaranda, too delicate to be built on, had to be protected, and raising the floor was one of many strategies employed during the build to protect it

The combination living and sleeping pod is linked via a chunky hallway to the kitchen and dining area. Partially illuminated by the all-day orange glow from Weir's trademark coloured skylight above the adjacent bathroom, this transition zone and of course the bathroom itself, exist in boisterous contrast with the otherwise muted interior palette of natural and unrefined finishes.

The palette choice – natural plywood and polycarbonate sheeting in the workshop, and white paint in the living areas – delineates the intended use of the various spaces. By separating the structure into discrete spaces, the exterior forms also inform how the building is used. A gable-roofed cottage houses the living quarters while an attached corrugated iron shed, complete with skillion roof, is set aside for working.

So sharp it sparkles, the Exploding! Shed House demonstrates how the principles of good architectural design can exist unfettered by convention. The result is a solution for a contemporary lifestyle, where life is as much about work as work is about life. By referencing the history of the area, the architect has created a new narrative which despite drastically departing from local convention nevertheless sits happily amongst the buildings that were its inspiration.

Design Notes

/ Open floorplan and areas of different use are linked by polished concrete as the single floor material.

/ The bathroom is bathed in orange light from a coloured skylight – a deliberate contrast with the restrained colour palette of the remaining interior spaces.

/ While the plinth on which the living area sits was formed to protect the roots of a valued tree in the garden outside, it also determines the outer limits of the living area within the surrounding open-plan floor space.

OPPOSITE, TOP LEFT
White walls and charcoal aluminium joinery are the dominant colour motifs throughout the building. Grey linen bedding reflects this aesthetic.

TOP RIGHT
An industrially styled bathroom is given a playful touch with the insertion of a hot orange skylight and sliding door.

BOTTOM RIGHT
Simple modern furniture and occasional pops of colour are all that are needed to introduce liveliness into the interior.

BOTTOM LEFT
The open shelved kitchen units are inexpensively constructed from Formply – a slightly glossy surfaced, resin-impregnated plywood most commonly used for formwork in the concrete industry – while traditional butchers' tiling on the splashback and a Belfast sink allude to the fact that this is as much a work-space as it is a dwelling.

OVER PAGE
The studio and its attached washup area (cum laundry) is set at an angle to the living area, replicating that of the adjacent dining area. The lowered ceiling above the washup area is useful storage.

PAGE 68
The jacaranda in the front yard was protected at all stages of the building project. Recessing the front entrance to accommodate it was deliberately part of the design process.

Exploding! Shed House

60M² ACCOMMODATION + 30M² WORKSPACE

Mount Lawley, Perth, WA

David Weir Architects

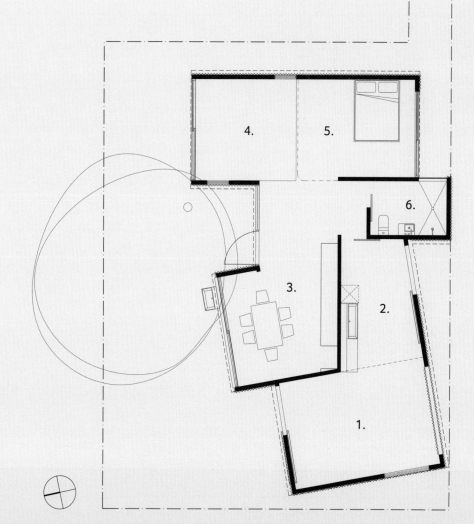

1   Studio
2   Laundry
3   Kitchen/Dining
4   Living
5   Bedroom
6   Bathroom

The Copper House

60M²

Coogee, Sydney, NSW

Takt | Studio for Architecture

Photography by
Shantanu Starick

Award

Australian Institute of
Architects 2015 NSW
Architecture Awards: The
Robert Woodward Award for
Small Project Architecture.

Like 'artisanal,' 'handmade' is a bit of a buzzword, but both terms accurately describe the little house floating like a butterfly high on the Coogee headland. Known as The Copper House, it is the closest thing possible in this day and age to a structure largely constructed, and certainly finished, by hand.

Hardly surprising then is that the name of the architectural practice responsible derives from the Latin root word which has evolved into 'tactile' in English. Takt's Brent Dunn is happy to acknowledge it is a term that deeply informs their work. 'Takt comes from the Latin *tactilis* and it means a number of things that are very important to us – sense of touch, music, time, metre and measure.'

Important too was sharing client Jeremy Godwin's admiration for Zen Buddhist design, and their similar tastes and values. As a personal friend, Godwin already knew what drove Dunn and his colleague Katherina Hegel's work. 'I was looking for style, simple elegance and function and I knew they were the people to do it.'

Renovating the existing fibro shack was not an option. Built straddling the boundary line, it was also falling down, with little more than 'paint and asbestos patches', holding it together. Demolition was the only sensible course of action.

A steep, skinny building platform with limited access and privacy issues was revealed. Even though the client only envisaged a 60m² structure, acheiving that goal was not without its challenges. Regulations required a 900mm setback from the boundaries and issues around privacy – both requirements further constrained what was possible.

Dunn and Hegel's solution was to design using the concept of the descending musical scale, and to detail it with the purity of the Zen Buddhist aesthetic. The result overcame the narrowness of the site while also maximising views and sunlight for both it and its neighbours, and importantly, it was a design that could be constructed almost entirely by hand – necessary because the narrow access around the worksite meant everything had to be handled manually.

PREVIOUS PAGE
The descending cascade of butterfly roofs and the weathered copper exterior have a note of Zen purity about them.

OPPOSITE
The pavilion to the rear of the site – and highest up the hill – houses the living area and leads directly to a small rear courtyard. Prioritising privacy rather than views in this way was a deliberate strategy that prevented overlooking neighbouring properties.

The agility of the form and the romantic tactility of the finishes throughout are impossible to ignore

OPPOSITE, TOP LEFT
The narrow, steep site required the building to be constructed without the use of anything more than lightweight tools. All materials and structural elements (such as windows, doors and roof trusses) had to be either constructed onsite or carried up the hill by manpower.

TOP RIGHT
Floor to ceiling glazing and lines of high level clerestory windows are some of the strategies enabling light to reach all parts of the interior. Bars of opaque film placed horizontally across the upper parts of the windows alongside the side boundaries provides privacy for both the neighbours and the inhabitants.

BOTTOM
While not large, the living room feels spacious because of the light entering from three sides and the direct access to the courtyard at the rear.

The decision to interlock three butterfly-roofed pavilions and to step them down the hillside, granting each one unobstructed views and sunlight through the asymmetrically positioned valley in the roof of the one below, was central to the design. Dunn points out that while this solution made the most of the views, just as importantly in a mere 60m² of space, it also meant that the 'spaces never feel confined, and that a sense of the interior and exterior knitting together was possible.' By subtly increasing the stud height and dimensions of the boxes as they step upwards towards the rear, each one not only acknowledges the contour of the land beneath, but also illustrates the increasing social importance of each function – the ascending order being second bedroom, master bedroom and then living and eating.

Introducing light from every angle through a combination of window types and positions – boxed bays to the front, clerestories along the roofline, louvres for controllable ventilation – visually expands volume despite the comparative narrowness of the spaces. So too does the slight over-sailing of each pavilion over the next. Practically, this device allows for an unusual amount of storage but it also provides a seamless connection between each structure.

With the two front pavilions housing bedrooms, and the larger one at the rear reserved for living, cooking and dining, the liveability of the interior is unquestionable, and the smallness of the footprint is hardly an issue. The agility of the form and the romantic tactility of the finishes throughout are impossible to ignore.

The eye-catching asymmetry of the butterfly roofs is just the start of it. Blessed with a client whose accountant made it possible, every single element is in effect handmade or hand applied. Copper sheeting, gently weathering to a soft green, clads the exterior and bathroom's interior, panels of gesso-sealed artists canvas covers many interior walls, and indigo concrete floors are hand polished with liquefied beeswax. Everything, whether small like door handles made from leather bicycle handle grips or large like much of the furniture being assembled or built on-site, is touched by human endeavour.

The result is astonishing. As much installation as habitation, its owner sees it as 'a tranquil, pleasurable place'. The architects, meanwhile, are looking forward to visiting it in fifty years. 'It will be a lovely place to return to.'

Design Notes

/ Formed as three distinct but connected pavilions, the building makes best use of an extremely steep and narrow site.

/ Descending butterfly roofs permit all day winter sun, as well as wide, unobstructed views from all levels.

/ The artisanal character of much of the construction is apparent in the application of handworked copper sheeting as exterior cladding and for interior bathroom waterproofing, stretched canvas for internal wall coverings and handbuilt furniture.

OPPOSITE, TOP
One of the two minimally inspired bedrooms is dramatised by deep timber-clad window reveals. Concealed storage along one wall disappears in the depths of a 'functional' wall.

BOTTOM
Intersecting angles and opposing light sources, plus the ability to look out to the wide view across the valley of the roof below, gives the small kitchen a magic that its size belies.

OVER PAGE
The horizontal lines produced by louvre windows and stairs are a repeating theme throughout.

The Copper House

60M²

Coogee, Sydney, NSW
Takt | Studio for Architecture

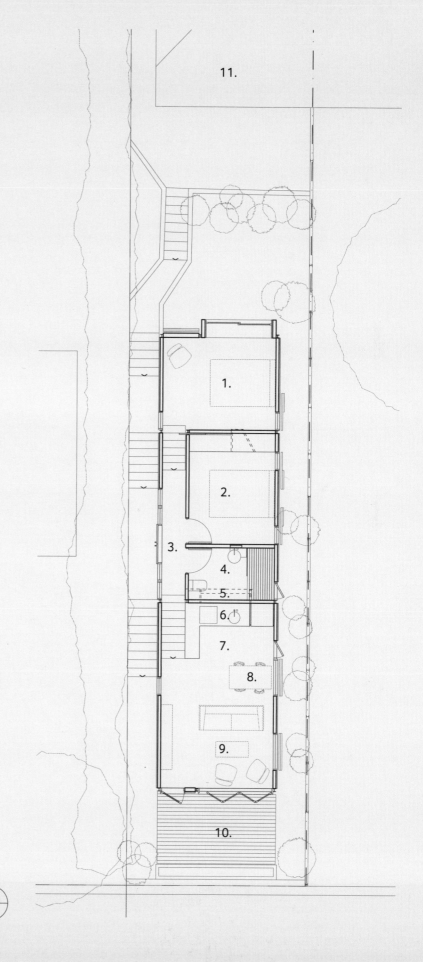

Mount Lawley House

70M² ACCOMMODATION
(+ OFFICE AND ANCILLARY ACCOMMODATION)

Mount Lawley, Perth, WA

Robeson Architects

Photography by
Dion Robeson

Award

Australian Institute of
Architects 2015 WA
Architecture Awards:
Commendation for Small
Projects Architecture

Setting up as a young architect is a daunting task. Having the skill
set and education is one thing – but it's quite another to convince
a potential client of an assured outcome when there's nothing out
there that proves you've got what it takes. Simone Robeson knew
that self promotion in the form of a successful and high profile
project was essential. To this end, she had identified a vacant plot
on a busy street corner which, despite its high profile position,
no-one seemed to want. 'It had been on the market for a year and
because it had so many constraints it was relatively inexpensive.
Even so it was scary, but it was just what I wanted – it had visibility
and it was affordable. I knew it was a unique opportunity, but I also
knew it wasn't going to be easy.'

Constraints are what architects call problems. This site
had problems galore, the most immediate being that not all its
diminutive 180m² was usable. A 1.5m wide sewer easement along
its long rear boundary, and the oblique triangular shape of the
front outer corner meant these areas were either unbuildable or
of limited use.

Fortunately, the local authority wanted a good quality building
on this very visible site and Robeson was given help to navigate
the unavoidable departures from the usual stringent regulations.
'I needed to maximise the use of the site to make it pay its way,
so I had to be able to use it flexibly, even though it's zoned for
residential use only. Residential upstairs, where I could make my
home, with an office and ancillary accommodation downstairs.'

PREVIOUS PAGE
A dramatic response was required
due to the triangular shape of
this long vacant site. Any building
needed to reflect this to maximise
the building platform to its
fullest extent.

OPPOSITE
Slot windows placed deliberately
high direct the outlook toward the
trees in the adjacent park rather
than to the traffic below.

Robeson's design confirms the truth of the much-used adage: 'within constraints lie the best solution'

Fulfilling such a combination of requirements on such a constricted site obliged Robeson to make herself the most demanding of clients. 'I had to be really clever and really disciplined. Every aspect of the design had to work overtime. There was no room for indulgence, but neither was I prepared to produce something less than perfect – such a visible site deserved an outcome that did it justice, and which also demonstrated what I was capable of.'

Accepting that certain things couldn't be changed, Robeson used the striking outline of the block as her starting point. 'I wasn't trying to make a statement. It was a case of looking at the site, subtracting the sewer easement (regulations prohibit building over a public sewer line, and any neighbouring building has to be set back a prescribed distance from it) and then maximising the footprint as much as possible.'

The result is a crisp two-storeyed building with boldly experimental forms that replicate each other and the site beneath. Triangles are, for obvious reasons, the dominant motif, with the leading apex reproduced, albeit softened into a wedge, in the outer perimeter fencing. The local authority required that the lower storey be set back from the street frontage of the site. Although this meant the footprint of this level had to be reduced, it added a design dimension in that the upper storey appears to float. The effect is that of the sails of a yacht overshadowing the body of the boat below. Reinforcing this impression is the use of white paint for the upper storey, juxtaposed against the receding depths of the exposed sand-faced brick cladding of the lower level.

Carefully placed windows punctuate both levels of the facade and, because of the very public position, sightlines were drawn to ensure privacy where needed. The requirements of both levels are addressed in ways specific to their needs. One-way glass in the protruding steel box on the lower level allows it to function as a private people-watching zone and light source. Slot windows placed deliberately high in the living room above permit views of the treetops of a nearby park but prevent the space from being overlooked by neighbouring houses. Despite the extra expense, heat and noise-minimising high tech glazing was used throughout to reduce overheating from the north and west and to reduce traffic noise.

OPPOSITE, TOP
Although wide at the end where the kitchen is situated, the living room narrows along its length towards the apex formed by the corner of the site.

BOTTOM RIGHT
A small triangular balcony is the dramatic culmination of the building's form.

BOTTOM LEFT
Wrapping the stairwell with a continuous piece of glass makes a dramatic statement externally while filling the interior with light.

86

The accommodation on the first floor is crisp and minimal. Burnished concrete floors, white walls and custom-designed furnishings present an uncluttered and deceptively spacious face to the world. The near invisible positioning of the stairwell buffers the bedroom and bathroom from the living area. By minimising circulation in such a way, while simultaneously delighting the eye with snatched views and multiple light sources, Robeson has enabled a small, unconventionally shaped space to function far above its pay grade.

Robeson's design confirms the truth of the much-used adage: 'within constraints lie the best solution'. She also demonstrates that quality and innovation can be delivered on a budget, and that even the most unpromising sites are never unusable. All they need is imagination.

Design Notes

/ The triangular form of the building makes best use of the site and the geometric angles become the defining design motif.

/ Both interiors and exteriors rely on form rather than decorative detailing for impact – finishes are crisply minimal and references industrial.

/ Built-in furniture makes best use of the awkward corners – most items have a secondary function as storage.

OPPOSITE, TOP
A sliding door gives privacy to the bedroom from the staircase that separates it from the living space. When privacy is not required it remains open, allowing wide views of the sky and park through the window that wraps the stairwell.

BOTTOM
A black, white and grey colour scheme, and an unobtrusive material palette, effect the restraint necessary in a space dominated by the drama of its form.

OVER PAGE
Despite being on a busy junction, traffic noise is minimised by heavyweight materials and double glazing.

Mount Lawley House

<u>70M² ACCOMMODATION</u>
<u>(+ OFFICE AND ANCILLARY ACCOMMODATION)</u>
Mount Lawley, Perth, WA
Robeson Architects

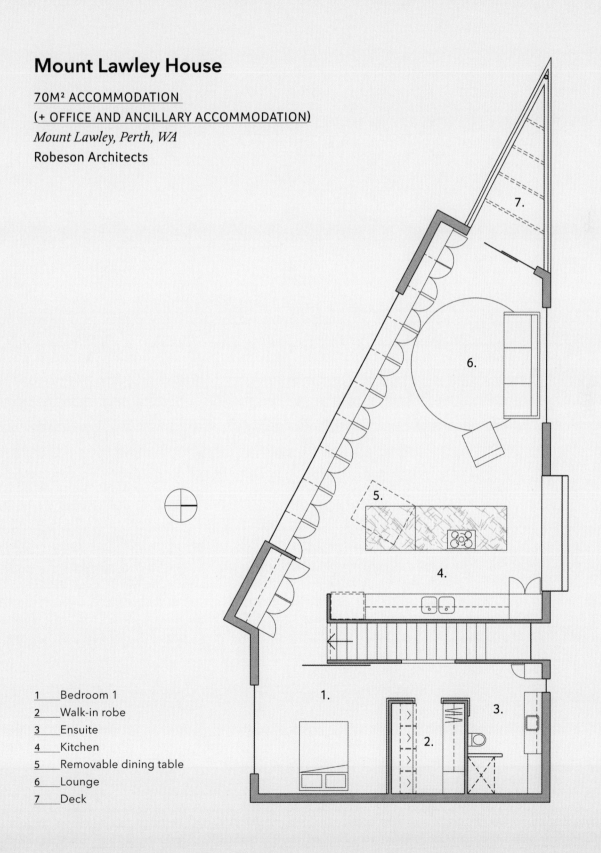

<u>1</u>   Bedroom 1
<u>2</u>   Walk-in robe
<u>3</u>   Ensuite
<u>4</u>   Kitchen
<u>5</u>   Removable dining table
<u>6</u>   Lounge
<u>7</u>   Deck

#thebarnTAS

38M² + 24M² MEZZANINE

/ *CBD, Hobart, TAS*

workbylizandalex

Photography by
Sean Fennessy

Awards

National Institute of
Architects Awards 2015
National Architecture Awards:
Nicholas Murcutt Award for
Small Project Architecture
and National Award for
Heritage

Horses once lived in the sandstone barn that Liz Walsh and Alex Nielsen fell in love with. Built around 1829 as stabling for an adjacent inn, so little had changed when the owners found it that mangers, stalls and heaps of decaying grain sacks were still in place. There was even a faint whiff of long-departed horse in the air.

Walsh and Nielsen could see past all that. With the honed eyes of recently graduated architects they were entranced by everything about it – the exposed and rugged roof timbers, the weathered brick and sandstone that formed its 400mm walls and the patina of age on the worn timbers. It was not only the materials that appealed. Equally important was the historical context. Everything was clearly handmade – most probably by convict labour – a heritage Nielsen and Walsh felt deserved recognition and protection.

The fact that everything, interiors and structure alike, were in an advanced state of dilapidation mattered not a jot. 'We knew from the moment we first climbed over the wall what it could be,' remembers Walsh. 'It was small enough not to be daunting, and the location only moments from the centre of Hobart couldn't be better. And it was beautiful!'

The bank, however, did not share their confidence and finance was hard to secure. Eventually, plans drawn by Walsh and Nielsen convinced the lending team that a workable two-bedroom home could be created within the tight footprint and despite the steeply pitched 45° roofline. A strict one year build-time was imposed but they were given the necessary funds to proceed.

PREVIOUS PAGE
Attention has been drawn to the simple barn-like form with the simplicity of the window joinery that flanks the original door. The surrounding 5mm shadow gap is a deliberate strategy to point out the difference between old and new.

OPPOSITE
An oversized pivoting door – the only major structural change – accesses a small courtyard garden with views out over the wider neighbourhood.

OPPOSITE, TOP LEFT
Looking through the pivoting door
from the courtyard it is possible
to imagine how dark the interior
would have been without it.

TOP RIGHT
The living area is enclosed below
the floor of the mezzanine above
it. The patina of wear on the worn
bricks and the exposed joists
contrast with the sleek surface
of the new floor.

BOTTOM RIGHT
The main bedroom on the
mezzanine above the living area
is dramatically surrounded by
the restored beams of the steeply
pitched roof.

BOTTOM LEFT
A study alongside the bedroom
on the mezzanine, situated below
the angles of the roof, looks out
through an internal window across
the void above the dining area to
the view beyond.

The floorplan is a masterpiece of economy with living, dining, spare-bedroom alcove and bathroom on the ground floor, and main bedroom and study on the mezzanine above. The biggest structural change was the insertion of a large, pivoting glazed door into the north facing facade – a change that allowed a necessary connection with what became a small enclosed courtyard. Not only does this flood the interior with light but it also visually extends the adjacent dining area into the courtyard itself and directs the view from the living room outwards as much as the void above the room carries it up.

The crisply contemporary joinery was a deliberate strategy – one that Nielsen saw as '… quite simple. [We aimed to] to retain as much of the existing building fabric as possible. Where services and amenity were required we provided new insertions – but it was important that these be read differently to what already existed. By doing so, the past and present have space to breathe.' Thus, windows, minimally framed in contrast to the heft of venerable timber doors and the staircase to the mezzanine – all seem to float a few millimetres apart from the original fabric of the structure around them.

The living and dining areas are connected, but with the dining area intimately enclosed below the ceiling of the extended arm of the mezzanine, and the void above the living area reaching all the way to the underside of the timber roof four metres above, the mood in each is very different. Playing with volume was another strategy to inject diversity into the tight floorplan and although the area of the living room is smaller than its vertical volume, the drama conferred by the roof structure distracts and entertains to such an extent this is immaterial.

A central service core, monumentally scaled despite its compact surroundings, completes the ground floor. Intended, in a design sense, as a device to draw the eye upwards, this also has the practical function of containing the kitchen and bathroom within handsome timber joinery while providing a large storage area on the mezzanine above. Concealing essential functions so thoroughly reminds one how important the primary functions of eating and relaxing were in the design process. Walsh recalls 'it was always non-negotiable that we had room to entertain twenty. This is a small space, but we were never prepared for it to feel mean, and it doesn't have to.'

We knew from the moment we first climbed over the wall what it could be

To keep the bank happy, a second sleeping area in the form of a small sleeping-nook – or second living room – lies semi-concealed behind this central core. As #thebarnTAS is now primarily in use as short term accommodation, this extra sleeping space has widened the appeal and usefulness of the space. '[You could call it] a successful example of the architect as investor model,' comments Walsh.

No longer filled with the dust of century-old spider webs, this is a secret and romantic place. The sensitivity demonstrated in its restoration and repurposing won Nielsen and Walsh major architectural awards. It also shows that a dogged commitment to employing the best of contemporary architectural practice to restore historic structures can allow unappreciated gems such as this one to be enjoyed on a daily basis, while also being preserved for posterity.

Design Notes

/ Using volume, outlook and what Walsh and Nielsen describe as 'a clear materials strategy' defined spaces within a small footprint.

/ Respect for the heritage of this almost 200-year-old building was demonstrated through clearly demarking the difference between old and new elements with shadow lines and the use of colour.

/ An oversized, glazed pivoting door allows the courtyard to become a third living space, even when the weather does not permit its actual use.

OPPOSITE, TOP LEFT
Simple white bedlinen contrasts with the rugged texture of the sandstone wall at the head of the bed.

TOP RIGHT
The kitchen is located within a central service core. This has been deliberately designed to appear to be a piece of stand-alone furniture.

BOTTOM RIGHT
Carefully stacked firewood adds a further texture to the thick courtyard walls.

BOTTOM LEFT
Like many of the new joinery elements, the staircase hovers a few millimetres away from the fabric of the original structure, giving it what the architects describe as 'room to breathe'.

OVER PAGE
The weathered double door is the original that once let horses in and out of the building.

#thebarnTAS

<u>38M² + 24M² MEZZANINE</u>
CBD, Hobart, TAS
workbylizandalex

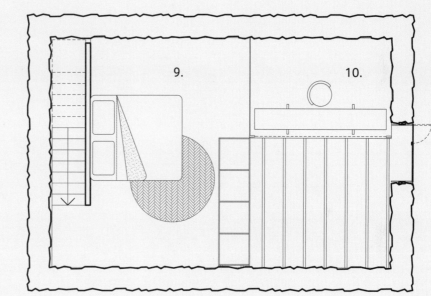

Upper floor

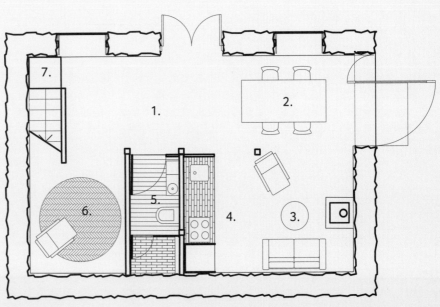

1   Entry
2   Dining room
3   Living
4   Kitchen and
      European laundry
5   Bathroom
6   Sitting room/
      Second bedroom space
7   Stair to mezzanine
8   Courtyard
9   Bedroom
10   Study

Ground floor

Niche XS House

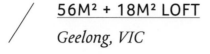

56M² + 18M² LOFT

Geelong, VIC

Small Change Design & Construction

Photography by
Sean Fennessy

Rarely is a company name so perfectly apt as to double as mission statement, but Small Change Design & Construction is an exception, with a bold statement of intent delivered with small, well-executed stand-alone dwellings for substantially less than $200,000 (excluding land).

Now home to very happy first-home buyer, builder and designer Sally Wills' first foray into small, predesigned (but not prebuilt) homes, it embodies her belief that high-quality housing can be both affordable and sustainable, and what's more, answers a cross-generational need for housing of this sort. 'When I was marketing this house for sale, we were inundated with enquiries from first-time buyers and downsizers in almost equal proportions. Both demographics are convinced that living in small, well-designed, more affordable spaces is the way forward. Perhaps there's a feeling that living better with less is more a liberation than a penance.'

Wills continues to lobby the Victorian State Government to relax the rules around the construction of secondary dwellings; she would like Victoria to adopt similar protocols to those which have been in place in NSW since 2009. 'The NSW model has demonstrated that $100,000–200,000 builds are viable, both as long term rental stock and small owner-occupied homes. I know that when the rules change in Victoria I will be busy as I have a list as long as my arm waiting to build.'

The footprint of Wills' Niche XS is a mere 56m², not including the 18m² mezzanine loft which, although not classified as 'habitable space', is used as storage and occasional overflow guest quarters. Every aspect of its design, an example of which is the asymmetrical roofline which pitches 42 degrees to the north and 26 degrees to the south, works overtime. A contemporary and slightly quirky twist on the traditional suburban gable roof, this roofline also allows the placement of correctly orientated solar panels for hot water if an off-grid option is required.

Whimsical or not, details like this are deliberate. Wills admits she was determined to design something that sat well within a suburban environment. 'Hard edged modernism has its place, but for an affordable solution with a mass-market appeal, hip and gable roofs work very well. The extra detail they afford removes any hint of blandness.'

PREVIOUS PAGE
Reflecting the roofline commonly found on suburban houses was a deliberate design choice, as was mixing horizontally grooved cypress sheet material with vertically grooved fibre cement board. All work to produce a building at home in its suburban surroundings, but with a contemporary twist.

OPPOSITE
The loft, while not classified as 'habitable space', is fully functional as overflow guest accommodation and storage.

104

Perhaps there's a feeling that living better with less is more a liberation than a penance

The same is true of the playful variation of materials and colour for the cladding, and the cleverly calculated interruptions in both vertical and pitched elements. The palette is surprisingly complex for such a modest structure. Golden toned, horizontally fixed, Frencham Cypress cladding gives street appeal to the west facade, while charcoal painted, vertically-grooved fibre cement board (FCB) wraps the northerly aspect. Recessing the entrance point and enclosing it below an open overhang of the roof adds further interest and complexity.

The interior layout is as considered as the exterior. With not a metre to spare, bathroom and bedroom tuck into the enclosed space below the mezzanine, and a wall of built-in cupboards in the bedroom allows the remainder of the compact footprint to remain uncluttered. Wall-to-ceiling kitchen storage is likewise contained in this area, and a thoughtfully detailed island unit removes any hint of mass-market oversimplification. The living area beyond is airy and welcoming with the tented ceiling allowed by the gable roof rising to a generous five metres at the ridge line. A bank of north-facing doors, sheltered and cooled in summer by the shade of a large deciduous tree, give onto a small, private yard.

Ultimately, a dwelling as perky, as downright sassy, as the Niche, succeeds because it wears its heart on its sleeve. It doesn't try to be anything more than it is, and what it is, is very good indeed.

Design Notes

/ The combination of an asymmetric gable roof with horizontally-fixed Frencham Cypress tongue and groove board cladding and vertically-grooved FCB reflects the suburban environment while introducing a contemporary twist.

/ Careful site orientation, along with the heat sink properties inherent in the polished concrete floor, minimises the need for heating and cooling.

/ Locating a large mezzanine loft above the bedroom, bathroom and kitchen encourages a sense of intimacy to these service areas while providing private space for guest accommodation, secondary living and storage.

OPPOSITE, TOP LEFT
The cathedral ceiling rises to 5m at its highest point, and encourages a sense of airy spaciousness within the small footprint.

TOP RIGHT
A plumbed-in island unit separates the living and dining area from the service areas to the rear.

BOTTOM RIGHT
The bathroom is generous in size and has ample storage.

BOTTOM LEFT
Slot windows above the bed and a built-in storage wall combine to make the bedroom both light and clutter-free.

OVER PAGE
Double doors into the yard produce outdoor flow similar to suburban houses much larger than this one.

Niche XS House

<u>56M² + 18M² LOFT</u>
Geelong, VIC
Small Change Design & Construction

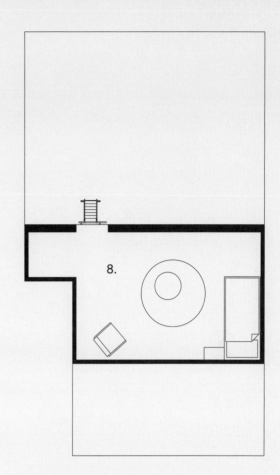

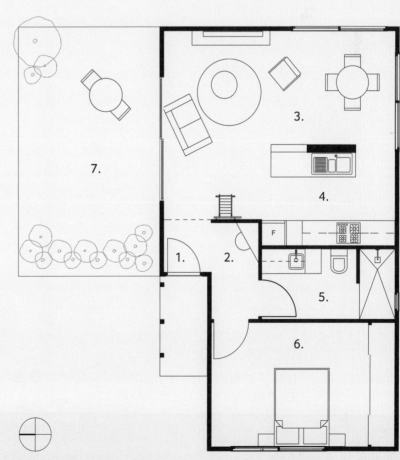

<u>1</u>   Entry
<u>2</u>   Study
<u>3</u>   Living/Dining
<u>4</u>   Kitchen
<u>5</u>   Bath/Laundry
<u>6</u>   Bedroom
<u>7</u>   Outdoor living
<u>8</u>   Storage loft

Woolloongabba gardenhouse II

80M²

Woolloongabba, QLD

REFRESH* DESIGN

Photography by
Roger D'Souza

Architects of jewel-box architecture are not always known for their hard-headed approach to the financial realities of property ownership. Indeed, their focus is often on beauty rather than budgets. It would be easy to assume that a structure as refined and thoughtful as the recently completed secondary dwelling in the back garden of a Woolloongabba cottage is the result of an expensive preoccupation with aesthetics rather than pragmatism.

But REFRESH* DESIGN's Austrian-trained architects Monika Obrist and Erhard Rathmayr are more than mere aesthetes. They are realists as well. As Rathmayr points out, property ownership comes with a raft of drivers, both financial and functional. 'Statistics show Australian homeowners tend to move every seven years, usually because the home they own no longer accommodates them; it's too big or too small. But each time they move it costs on average $50,000 in stamp-duty, real-estate fees, removal costs, minor alterations and the like. Over a person's lifetime this equates to around $350,000. We see more and more people making this connection, hence they decide to build an amenity which adds value to the home they own, while at the same time making it possible to "age in place" when the time comes.'

Recognising this growing trend, Obrist and Rathmayr have made a name designing what they have branded as 'my gardenhouse'- refined, compact homes that make cost efficient use of the often underutilised back gardens of the wider Brisbane area. The example in Woolloongabba is a case in point. 'The brief was to produce an inexpensive yet beautiful granny flat - one that could be rented out, or extend accommodation for the family without having to go through the nuisance of alterations to the main house. We knew from other projects that by using cost-effective building materials with care, we could transfer the savings into design features. This is what we aimed to do here.'

PREVIOUS PAGE
Decorative trim running above the windows and doors expands the rhythm set up by the horizontal lines of the triple bank of louvre windows; the pattern in turn echoes that on the wallpaper in the living area; details such as this add complexity to what otherwise would be largely a simple oblong box.

OPPOSITE
The combined living, dining and kitchen opens directly to a secluded terrace which – being in use for most of the year – almost doubles the size of the living area.

112

We knew that by using cost-effective building materials with care, we could transfer the savings into design features

From the beginning, care was taken to minimise the impact of the 80m² addition to the suburban landscape – although intensification on this scale is encouraged in Queensland, insensitive application of the rules is not. In this instance, the land (fortunately north-facing) fell away below the original dwelling, making it logical to reduce bulk by semi-recessing the new structure into the hillside. Orientating what was visible towards the north further helped separate the new dwelling from the pre-existing structure.

Just as external separation was essential between the original and new dwellings, so too were well organised internal connections within the tight footprint of the gardenhouse itself. With two storeys, a stairwell between the bedrooms and bathroom on the upper level and the living spaces below was essential but cramped staircases are common in floorplans as tight as this. In this case, however, a narrow skin of silky black Formply, an unfussy profile for the stairs and an externally glazed wall have transformed what could have been a poky necessity into a stylish design feature in its own right.

The lower level is reserved for living. Facing north through a light canopy of greenery, this is an airy and elegant space. Its roomy feel is enhanced by more sleight-of-hand and eye. The kitchen island morphs into dining table, the laundry tucks into the powder room, and polished concrete floors encourage interiors and exteriors to flow seamlessly into each other. The impression of a single large living-area is furthered by glazing, bi-fold doors and high level louvres, to separate the indoor and outdoor spaces.

OPPOSITE, TOP
The pattern on the wallpaper at the rear of the living area was the inspiration behind the decorative theme that appears in various guises throughout the house.

BOTTOM
The location of the galley kitchen makes it equally accessible for both indoor and outdoor entertaining.

Queensland's hot and humid climate required that special attention be paid to achieving temperature stability, particularly in the summer months. The insulating mass of concrete to the rear, and the greenery in the courtyard to the fore, protected the lower level from temperature extremes. The upper level required a more considered strategy, especially on the exposed northern and eastern facades. Aluminium screens, laser cut in a geometric pattern which replicates that of the feature wallpaper in the living room below, control heat and glare, while adding visual interest and texture to the most visible flanks of the building. The motif recurs in the privacy screen on the bathroom window, connecting the upper and lower spaces, and the interior and exterior worlds.

Far more than the sum of its parts, the resulting structure is as eloquent as a picture book. Its narrative is gentle, quietly pointing out how intensification, even in the leafiest of suburbs, can enrich far more than it threatens.

Design Notes

/ Privacy is achieved by partially recessing the gardenhouse into the hillside between the two dwellings and orientating its living area to face outwards towards the rear of the block.

/ Inexpensive building products – concrete block, compressed fibre cement cladding, plywood (both traditional timber versions and resin-coated Formply), and corrugated iron – are used imaginatively as design statements as much as building materials.

/ Laser cut, powder coated aluminum screens replicate the pattern on the wallpaper in the living area. Dual function, they control excess light while simultaneously adding interest to the exterior facade.

OPPOSITE, TOP AND BOTTOM
Etched glass privacy panels in the main bedroom and bathroom repeat the motif from the living room wallpaper to produce privacy without reducing the amount of light. Charcoal aluminium joinery and black Formply cabinets contrast with white walls and simple furnishings.

OVER PAGE
Formply is used to replace the more traditional forms of balustrading, thus simultaneously saving space in a tight stairwell and making a style statement.

Woolloongabba gardenhouse II

80M²
Woolloongabba, QLD
REFRESH* DESIGN

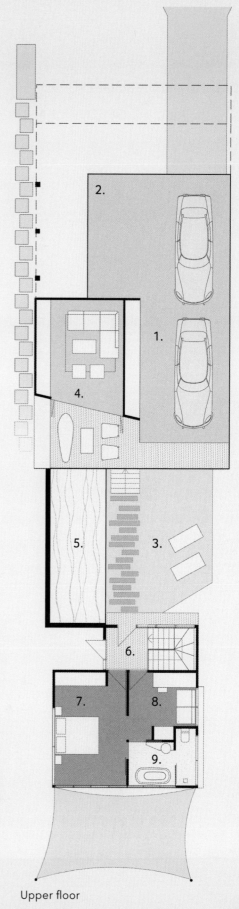

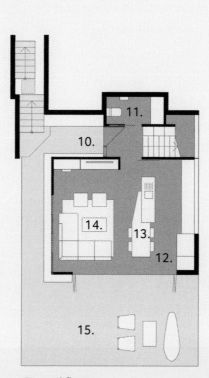

1   Joint garage
2   Undercroft
3   Joint outdoor area
4   Future lounge and deck
5   Future pool
6   Landing
7   Main bedroom
8   Bedroom/Study
9   Bath
10   Entry
11   Powder/Laundry
12   Kitchen
13   Dining
14   Living
15   Terrace

Ground floor   Upper floor

The Lighthouse

88M² (WORKSHOP NOT INCLUDED)

Hobart, TAS

Room11

Photography by
Jonathan Wherrett

About 8000 years ago the first known courtyard house was constructed on the banks of the Jordan river. Stone built on a monumental scale, it survives to this day. Dwellings with walls enclosing a central area made sense when predators abounded, and every culture that forsook the nomadic life for an agrarian existence developed a version of it. Variations were many, but what all had in common was a central area, open to the sky in part and enclosed by buildings and walls in others.

Lee and Marc Prince's courtyard house on its tight urban block did not require protection from maneating beasts or invading warriors. Rather, the need for enclosure came from those twenty-first century invaders – overlooking neighbours and noise pollution. A garden subdivision, it was surrounded by other properties. As is often typical of inner city infill sites of this nature, while it enjoyed proximity and location, it was less than ideal in other respects.

Megan Baynes and Thomas Bailey, from local architectural practice Room11, were not intimidated by the limitations, and Bailey recalls how they knew from the beginning '… we needed a perimeter strategy that worked for this site. It wasn't overlooked from the street, but it was overlooked by neighbours on all sides. Designing a house around a courtyard was the obvious solution.'

It was a resolution embraced wholeheartedly by the clients. Lee Prince recounts, 'We had great respect for their work and knew we shared an aesthetic sensibility and [because of that] we had complete confidence in their ability to deliver something special. They listened to us. They heard what we wanted.'

What was wanted was '… a small, modern, light, warm house – one that was affordable to us and acceptable to the neighbours'. The budget was tight and the site swampy, but like all constraints, these had a way of disciplining the design rather than compromising it.

PREVIOUS PAGE
The courtyard faces north-east and bi-fold plywood doors alongside the kitchen area can be pulled across the glazed sliding doors behind them until the right amount of shade has been achieved.

OPPOSITE
Fully enclosed, the courtyard is a private space that virtually doubles the footprint of the living area.

**It wasn't overlooked from the street, but it was
overlooked by neighbours on all sides. Designing
a house around a courtyard was the obvious solution**

Unstable subsoil meant a floating insulated slab was the
obvious place to start. Shaped like an 'L', it wraps the long southerly
and shorter easterly boundaries, with the longer arm containing the
living, kitchen and dining areas, and the shorter the two bedrooms.
The resultant north-north-westerly oriented lee of the building
serves as an outdoor extension to the living area it shelters.

The separation between the indoor and outdoor spaces
is deliberately permeable, with large retractable glass doors
alongside the living area and smaller timber bi-folds beside the
kitchen allowing the two zones to operate as one. When all are
open, the modest dimensions of the interior expand in a seamless
progression between light and shadow, shade and shelter.

Privacy for the master bedroom was achieved by making the
courtyard wall in this area solid, while a small private decked area,
accessible only through glazed doors from the bedroom itself on its
northern facade, warms and lights it.

A small utility hub to the rear of the kitchen connects the rear of
the 'L' to the second bedroom and these, together with the master
bedroom, form the easterly perimeter of the structure. A workshop
is situated on the westerly corner, and high fences and a retractable
gate enclose the remaining two sides of the courtyard.

OPPOSITE, TOP
Open shelving in the kitchen is an
attractive but inexpensive way to
create storage.

BOTTOM RIGHT
Cladding around the entry area
is in the same material as the
adjacent courtyard wall, while
the doors that lead from this area
are glazed to allow light into the
workshop and westerly light into
the living area.

BOTTOM LEFT
The seating area of the living space
has triple aspect light sources – the
service yard at the rear is glimpsed
through this window.

124

OPPOSITE, TOP LEFT
A simple yet elegant bathroom services bedrooms to either side of it. Locating the toilet separately means there is no inconvenience when guests stay over.

TOP RIGHT
The master bedroom has its own private courtyard and is lit through the wall of sliding doors that give onto it.

BOTTOM
The courtyard off the master bedroom opens to the main courtyard on its westerly side. Timber decking denotes the line between the public and private spaces.

OVER PAGE
High walls are constructed from a combination of stacked concrete block (where the adjacent road is busiest) and fibre cement board. The contrasting textures add complexity even when the colour palette is particularly restrained.

None of the spaces are large, but as Bailey explains, all appear more generous than they are, partly by the volume allowed by their 2.7m ceiling height, and also because of their connection either to the courtyard, or through skylights, to the sky itself. 'You could describe it as sleight-of-hand, because it is a small house, but every area in it appears large. For example, the bathroom is a small vertical space, but because you can lie in the bath and look up at the stars it feels anything but. It's about finding an appropriate character for each space.'

Bailey goes on, describing it as '… a crisp, humble, house in an urban sea'. It might be a small house, modest in scale and uncomplicated in design, but for its owners it has been, 'little short of life changing'.

Design Notes

/ The high walls of the courtyard grant privacy and shelter, while the inner glazed wall between it and the living area allow both to operate seamlessly as one large space.

/ Glazed wall between courtyard and living room, skylights in the utility area and sliding doors from bedrooms onto private decks fill the interior with light.

/ Utility areas are deliberately small in order to allow a generously sized living area and two bedrooms on a small footprint.

The Lighthouse

88M² (WORKSHOP NOT INCLUDED)

Hobart, TAS

Room11

1	Entry
2	Lounge
3	Dining
4	Kitchen
5	Bedroom
6	WC
7	Store/Laundry
8	Bathroom
9	Deck
10	Patio
11	Workshop

Tourmaline Pavilion

69M²

Narrabeen, Sydney, NSW

Peter Stutchbury Architecture

Photography by
Michael Nicholson

Most children dream of sleeping under the stars, and many a suburban garden will have played home to a tent and a few excited children. Shona Veney and her children sleep in the nearest thing – they live in a pavilion in the garden of her parents' home.

Pavilion architecture appeared on the Australasian architectural scene about fifteen years ago, and immediately found its place in the language of the beach house. Casual yet refined, witty and light-footed, it dances the tightrope of reducing what could be complicated to the elemental – successfully meeting the need for shelter with the desire for beauty.

Veney needed both. A single mother living under her parents' roof, she was lovingly housed, but a separate but nearby home would give each family unit room to breathe, while still having proximity to the support of a multi-generational living arrangement. The idea of building something '… simple and primal, connected to nature' in the backyard took root.

Approaching Peter Stutchbury, Australian Institute of Architects gold medallist and all-round luminary in the architectural scene, to design the 60m² home permitted under NSW's secondary dwelling legislation was a bold move, but one that Veney never regretted. 'Everybody told me not to waste money on an architect … but I knew I couldn't, and shouldn't, design this by myself. [What they designed] has changed my life.'

For Stutchbury and his team, designing a small dwelling such as this was not difficult – stretching the less than $300,000 budget was. As Luke Pigliacampo, project architect to the job, comments, 'The budget was the major constraint of the project [and this] informed the thinking towards conventional building techniques. Through the evolution in the detailing it became an exercise in composition, and this approach created the architecture.'

PREVIOUS PAGE
Both sides of the central core open in the tent-like pavilion style of architecture that is both a casual and yet elegant way to link indoor and outdoor living spaces. External sliding doors were hung with the glazed areas below the solid timber panel. This unusual arrangement met regulatory requirements to provide visual privacy for neighbours.

OPPOSITE
The light glowing through the translucent polycarbonate band of clerestory windows running between the roof and doors gives the impression that the roof is supported by little more than light.

132

There's a strong feeling of being protected and secure, without being disconnected from the outside world

The resulting elegance and simplicity is deceptive. Blessed with a flat site and a north-south orientation, a skillion roofed pavilion, opening tent-like to the north and south through a lightly constructed central core, made the most of the space available. Being open to the rear, however, compromised the privacy of its neighbours. Inspired lateral thinking – what Pigliacampo refers to as 'using the conventional in unconventional ways' – created art out of necessity. The most obvious example is installing the external, semi-glazed doors upside-down so that the timber section acts as an eye-level screen. By doing this the outlook is directed down into the garden itself rather than up towards the neighbours' windows, and yet light and ventilation is not compromised.

Standard building product dimensions were applied throughout, with the stud height of 2.4m determined by the size of the concrete-board cladding sheets, and highlight windows by the width of the multicell polycarbonate sheet with which they are glazed. Such dimensions minimised wastage, but the care taken in the detailing is what elevates this building above the ordinary. Inserting a line of translucent glazing between the roof edge and the top of window and door openings not only allows a generous volume to the interior, it also encourages the sweet notion that this is a 'floating' roof – as light a structure as is possible to be constructed.

Internally, the layout is as simple as would be expected in a tent. A lightweight central core is juxtaposed against the solidity of a pair of sheltering 'boxes' which house bedrooms at either end. Every spatial plane, as much as every centimetre of volume, has a function. Concealed storage keeps the spaces clutter-free, and the large expanses of glazing promote a sense of scale to the comparatively small interior.

Originally a 'complying development' of only 60m² the project did not require council consent and, like all buildings of this type, was approved within ten working days by an independent certifier. As it became apparent that accommodating three near adult-sized humans in that space would be a stretch, permission was obtained for a 9m² addition to increase the size and storage of the master bedroom, while the cube at the other end of the living core was divided into two bedrooms for the children.

Veney never ceases to marvel at the transformation her 'dream home' has made in her life. 'It's pivotal. I love absolutely everything about it. There's a strong feeling of being protected and secure, without being disconnected from the outside world.' Just like those childhood nights in a tent with the lights of home nearby.

Design Notes

/ A shared courtyard and lawn provides outlook and connection between the original and secondary dwellings.

/ A courtyard to the rear, accessed from the central core, allows for private outdoor living. When both sides of the core are open, the living spaces expand to include the gardens that frame it.

/ All bedrooms have direct access to the gardens through the sliding doors.

OPPOSITE, TOP LEFT
The two secondary bedrooms are small but with ample built-in storage are completely adequate.

TOP RIGHT
The indoor bathroom illustrated here is supplemented by an outdoor tub in the rear courtyard.

BOTTOM
The rear courtyard is a surprisingly spacious oasis of greenery.

OVER PAGE
The honeyed gold of hoop pine plywood lines the main bedroom – this extra space was added when it was decided both bedrooms at the other end of the house were needed for the children.

Tourmaline Pavilion

<u>69M²</u>
Narrabeen, Sydney, NSW
Peter Stutchbury Architecture

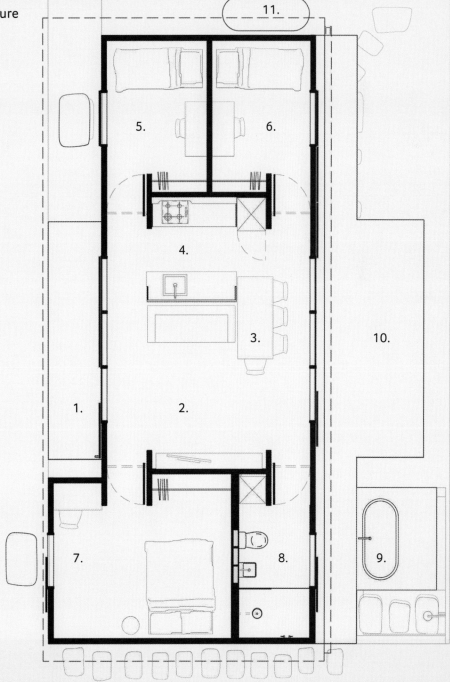

1   Entrance
2   Living area
3   Dining area
4   Kitchen
5   Bedroom 1
6   Bedroom 2
7   Master bedroom
8   Bathroom
9   Bath house
10 Private courtyard
11 Water tank

Hohnen House

<u>60M²</u>

Urunga, NSW

Self-Designed

Photography by
Daniel Dixon

Are small houses simple houses? Not usually. Are they affordable? Not always, and what might be small is all too often an expensive and exquisitely crafted box of ingenious problem-solving. Emma Hohnen's self-designed house on NSW's Mid North Coast is proof that simplicity, when done with wit and ingenuity, does not imply inadequacy.

Admittedly, Hohnen had some very specific motivations. Recently single and with a family to house, she was determined to take advantage of the regulations in NSW that allow 60m² secondary dwellings to be built in the gardens of existing housing. Careful planning was required, particularly in the site dimensions of any prospective purchase. A site with dual access, and a long narrow profile was crucial and it was these attributes that drew Hohnen to the property she now owns. 'It runs east to west, and the existing house sits well to the front. I could see it would be possible to site a small house in such a way that each dwelling could have privacy and adequate outdoor space.'

She was also realistic about what was achievable on her build budget of $100,000. 'I knew I had to keep the design as simple as possible, with an uncomplicated shape and roofline. I also knew that by using standard building material sizes I could prevent waste, and that there was always a place for recycled materials.'

Embodying Hohnen's liking for 'an uncomplicated, utilitarian look' her simple building is a triumphant blend of pragmatism and ingenuity. Oblong in shape, its 4.8m width was ultimately determined by the length of the bath and the size of the bedroom, 1700mm and 2900mm respectively, and the 12.5m length made up the 60m². Its jaunty skillion roof, thoughtfully applied horizontal colour bond cladding and generous glazing dispel any notion of unconsidered blandness. So too does the softening presence of a 50m² deck which connects the house to the raised garden beds that surround it.

PREVIOUS PAGE
The kitchen is quite literally the hub of the home with all activities taking place within metres of it.

OPPOSITE
A large covered deck blurs the boundaries between the cosiness of the indoor spaces and the lushness of the garden that surrounds it.

I wanted plenty of north-facing sun, high ceilings, open-plan living and clean lines

Despite the necessary simplicity of the form, light and space were non-negotiable, and in achieving these Hohnen was unwavering. 'I wanted plenty of north-facing sun, high ceilings, open-plan living and clean lines. These priorities were very clear to me from the start and they didn't change.' Even the position of the council sewer, which meant the house had to be situated as close to the northern boundary as possible, was not a disadvantage as it necessitated taking advantage of the best views to the south. A line of clerestory windows under the eaves of the northerly edge of the skillion roof cross-ventilate and illuminate throughout the year but limit direct sunlight, even in the height of the subtropical summer. Siting along this axis also permitted passive solar-gain from the south, with sunlight in winter reaching 4m into the 4.8m depth of the house. Combining these strategies minimised the need for additional heating and cooling – ceiling fans and louvre windows on the easterly facade are all that is required in summer to control temperature and humidity.

Timber bi-folds connect the open-plan living core to the decks and gardens and in the benign local climate these areas function as extensions to the living area itself. Although the combination of large living area and generous outdoor decks provided ample living space, planning regulations only permitted a single bedroom. But with two small children Hohnen needed a multi-functional space – somewhere the children could sleep, play and watch TV, and which could, on occasion, be used as an office for herself.

Her solution is typically ingenious. Unwilling to break the rules by building something permanent, she erected a solid but easily dismantled structure from off-the-peg chests-of-drawers and bookcases two-thirds of the way down the open reaches of the living room. Although not quite full-height, it encloses a private area which the children can call their own. The chests-of-drawers providing storage for their possessions are accessed from their side, while bookcases full of more general belongings face inwards into the living room.

OPPOSITE, TOP
Living in all its forms takes place in the central core of the simple oblong structure. The main bedroom and bathroom is at one end (out of shot), while a secondary sleeping and living area for the children is behind the book-lined room-divider at the far end.

BOTTOM RIGHT
Louvre windows mounted high on the long northerly wall provide cross ventilation and ample light throughout the year.

BOTTOM LEFT
The seating area of the living space is surrounded by books and personal possessions – many of them stored in the wall divider that divides this area from the children's space on the other side.

For Hohnen, building her home has been inspirational on many levels. 'There is something amazing about bringing the vision of a house you have designed into reality, and to see that it works. To be able to provide a home for my family and in an environmentally friendly way - I'd do it again in a heartbeat!'

Design Notes

/ Avoiding waste by using standard building material sizes and recycled materials where possible were key strategies to control the budget.

/ A skillion roof and horizontal colorbond cladding are an effective but sprightly response to a tight budget.

/ Constructing a wall from connected off-the-peg storage units – in this case bookcases and chests-of-drawers – provides storage for children's possessions on one side and wall space for electronics on the other.

TOP LEFT
The dining table is the multi-purpose centre of activity – it is where the family spend much of their time.

TOP RIGHT
Inexpensive fine gauge corrugated iron lines the simple bathroom.

BOTTOM RIGHT
The space carved off from the living room by the wall divider is large enough for a single bed and a desk for play and homework.

BOTTOM LEFT
Strategically placed mirrors help the small footprint feel bigger than it is.

OVER PAGE
The house is private behind high slatted fences, yet close enough for security and interaction with the main house.

Hohnen House

<u>60M²</u>
Urunga, NSW
Self-Designed

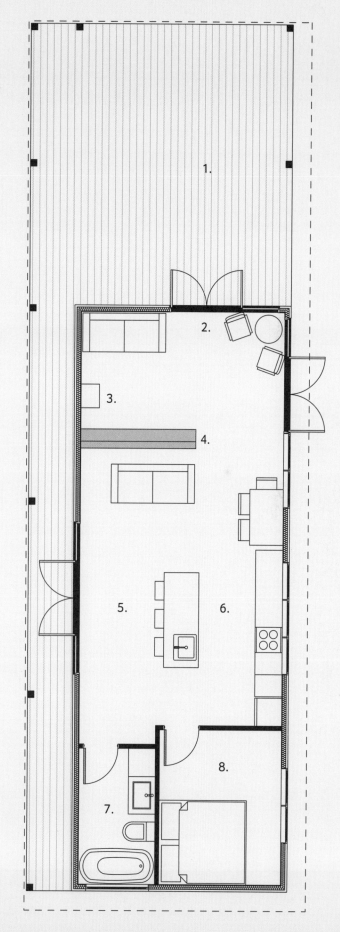

<u>1</u>____Deck
<u>2</u>____Entry
<u>3</u>____Wood burner
<u>4</u>____Divider/shelving
<u>5</u>____Living
<u>6</u>____Kitchen/Dining
<u>7</u>____Bathroom/Laundry
<u>8</u>____Master bedroom

Balnarring Retreat

/ 60M²

Balnarring, VIC

Branch Studio Architects

Photography by
Peter Clarke

Georgina Moore needed what Virginia Woolf once said no woman could do without; 'a room of one's own' – somewhere to dream, to plan, to create, above all, a space to simply be herself. The family property in heartland Victoria, blessed with a tranquil expanse of water surrounded by picturesque eucalyptus and bottlebrush, had plenty of land. What it needed was the room itself.

For Nicholas Russo, designing 'something small and flawless' for a client such as Moore, with the luxury of a spacious rural site to play with, was nothing less than a delight. With his practice more frequently engaged in larger scale urban architecture, he also saw it as an opportunity 'to aim for perfection. We had the space to build in the best possible position for the views – north across the water. Siting it like this also allowed it to feel very private from the main house, even though they are only minutes apart.'

The building not only faces north across the water, it is virtually in the water, with elegantly recessed concrete foundations lifting the front facade above the waterline so that it juts forward, almost like the prow of a ship. Unlike the marine industry's high tech polymers and plastics however, the rammed earth, polished concrete and dark stained timber of the exterior could not be more organic, embodying in their very essence what Russo sees as representing 'the needs not the finish. Nothing was intended to be smooth and artificial – everything had to be apparent.'

The same is true of the clear-finished, hoop pine plywood interior – an unadorned finish that exemplifies Russo's desire to 'design without artifice' although the concealed location of the bathroom, behind a door that appears to be a wall, somewhat contradicts this. Once behind the secret door it is an unexpectedly magical space, flooded with light from its glazed ceiling. Plumbing is handmade and surface mounted. Everything is tactile and refined, simultaneously exposed and concealed.

PREVIOUS PAGE
Vertically hung timber cladding is deliberately offset by the strong horizontal lines produced by the concrete footings and the low set slot windows.

OPPOSITE
Although apparently in an isolated setting the main dwelling on the property is close by across the gardens.

152

TOP LEFT
The bathroom has no windows but
is dramatically lit through its fully
glazed ceiling.

TOP RIGHT
A work space in front of one of the
slot windows has westerly views
across the gardens that separate
it from the main house, while
light pours in through the glazed
wall that looks out across the
tranquil water.

BOTTOM
A bedroom appears when the bed
is lowered from its concealed wall
alcove. The line in the ceiling above
allows a linen curtain to be drawn
for privacy if required.

OVER PAGE
Tranquillity was one of many
things the owner wanted in
this small house. Internally the
use of colour was deliberately
downplayed so as not to compete
with the external surroundings.
Flying Birds folded brass pendant
lamp was designed and made by
Nicholas Russo.

The main room too contains a multitude of secrets. Almost
every wall has hidden elements, each of which adds functionality
to what is, after all, still a small space. Handmade fittings, in brass
to match the sheet brass that encases the recessed kitchen alcove,
release plywood tables that fold down, shelves that appear and
disappear, lights that retreat or re-emerge depending on what the
need of the moment might be. The bed folds up into a recess at the
touch of a button and walls of inbuilt storage keep clutter at bay.

From the beginning Russo was keen to incorporate a sunken
daybed in the poured concrete floor at the glazed waterside
end of the structure. Although internal, this almost water level
viewing platform is a secluded space from which to interact with
nature, so private that even the paddling waterfowl through
the glass do not notice. In one of the many instances of onsite
development, plywood boxes were constructed to fill it when
not in use, extending the floor area and providing extra storage.
Lifted from the recess and grouped together, these boxes form a
daybed to enjoy views across the garden from the low-level window
alongside. Separately, they function as stools for visitors or, when
required, plinths for art or side tables for entertaining.

Positioning both the window alongside the daybed and its
partner across the room below eye level not only fills the interior
with low-level morning and evening light but also makes looking
in from outside difficult. Privacy was something Russo saw as
essential in a building whose main function is to offer a retreat.
'Once inside you have no idea that it's anywhere but alone in its
own little piece of landscape. Keeping these windows low means
you are the one that controls how much you see. They have the
added benefit of allowing the structure to be transparent across
its whole depth when viewed from outside … it comes across as
light and delicate.'

156

Everything is tactile and refined, simultaneously exposed and concealed

Delicate too is this tiny, refined treasure of a building. Not a thing unconsidered, nothing out of place, it exists as a personal and unique retreat from a sometimes less than perfect world.

Design Notes

/ The recess in the concrete floor can either be filled with plywood storage boxes to extend the floor area or, when empty, dressed with cushions as a sunken waterside daybed.

/ Various concealed, moveable elements such as fold-down beds and work tables, add multifunctionality to the small footprint.

/ Weighty materials (rammed earth and polished concrete) are leavened by a top-lit insert of polished brass in the kitchen alcove and a glazed roof in the bathroom.

OPPOSITE, TOP
Slot windows are inserted at exactly the same height on opposite sides of the building; deliberately low-set they are at the perfect height to look out from while seated inside, but are not easy to look into.

BOTTOM
Reflections and light play are as much part of the interior as the furnishings.

OVER PAGE
A recessed area in the concrete floor operates as a daybed close to the water.

Balnarring Retreat

<u>60M²</u>
Balnarring, VIC
Branch Studio Architects

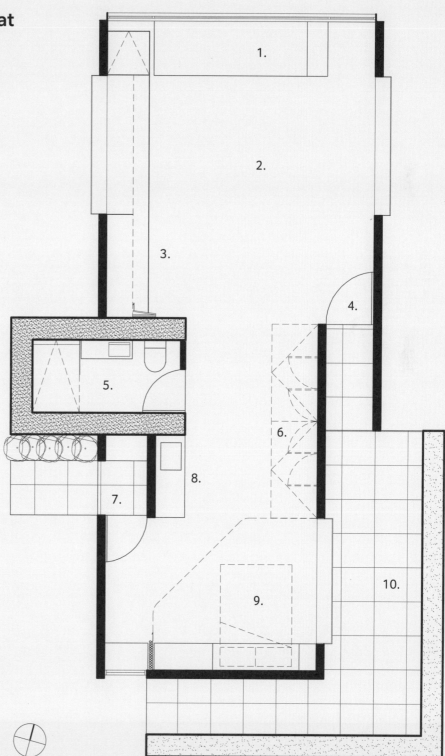

<u>1</u>	Daybed
<u>2</u>	Living
<u>3</u>	Study
<u>4</u>	Entry
<u>5</u>	Bathroom
<u>6</u>	Meals
<u>7</u>	Boots entry
<u>8</u>	Kitchen
<u>9</u>	Sleep
<u>10</u>	Terrace

Grass House

78M²

Fitzroy, Melbourne, VIC

David Luck Architecture

Photography by
Daniel Dixon

Awards
Australian Institute of
Architects 2016 Victorian
Architecture Awards:
Shortlisted for Sustainable
Architecture

163

Increasingly frustrated by what he sees as 'Australia's greedy spatial expectations', owner Ben Raphael never felt that his 47m² site was too small to be useful. 'When I said I was going to build here, friends told me it was too small, too awkward – that anything built on it would always be compromised – but the reality couldn't be further from the truth. It isn't large but I have everything I need.'

That 'everything' is contained within 78m² over two storeys. When compared to the 231m² of the average new built suburban home, it is small indeed, but its lack of size is offset by an abundance of attitude. With only a minimal setback, no off-street parking and a ziggurat-shaped upper level clad in grass-filled weathered COR-TEN steel planter boxes, it cuts a surprising sight amongst its heritage neighbours.

Architect David Luck's interpretation of local planning regulations was similarly unlikely. With a block about the size of a three garden sheds, building close to the site perimeters was essential, yet doing so appeared to contravene the required regulations for 5 per cent permeability and 20 per cent open green space.

The planning department of the local authority was an unlikely source of support – glad to see 'the most exciting building in years' making use of the tiny site. Nonetheless, the consent process was long and tortuous and the department's backing was invaluable. The intention was never to court controversy. As Luck points out, 'Sites like these require the most sensitive of neighbourhood responses, and the more rules broken, the less likely you are to get permission to proceed. Cladding the exterior with weathered steel planter boxes and filling them with grass mightn't seem the most obvious way of winning support, but by doing this we fulfilled the requirements for permeability and open green space. The building itself is, in effect, an eleven-metre-high shade tree.' Hidden at the rear are rainwater retrieval tanks that recycle the water collected from the roof to water the grasses.

PREVIOUS PAGE
COR-TEN steel planter boxes filled with native grasses are an eye-catching feature with a practical as well as decorative function – the plantings allow the building itself to meet the requirements for green space and permeability.

OPPOSITE
Virtually all the tiny 47m² corner site was permitted to be built over because of the green 'walls' and the water-catchment off the roof (into tanks in the rear yard).

There was also a need to avoid overshadowing the boundaries. This was achieved by recessing the upper storey back in a series of steps so that the silhouette is akin to a head of shaggy hair perched upon solid shoulders - an effect perhaps enhanced by the sunglasses effect of wrapping the outer corners with a pair of intersecting slot windows.

Internally the tight dimensions did not allow for a radical layout. Two bedrooms and a bathroom fill the ground floor. The second bedroom was only possible because the requirement for garaging was judged unnecessary in an area well serviced by public transport.

The entirety of the upper level is reserved for living, eating and cooking, and the spaces pop with energy. The inwardly pitched walls and obliquely slanting light, entering through the long slot windows which connect the sloping planes, render the interior form disjointed in an aesthetically pleasing way. Clouds scud across the glazed ceiling of the adjacent stairwell, and the outlook from the large window at the west-facing rear embraces the views of the neighbourhood as well. A small, semi-enclosed deck above the street is large enough to relax on, yet small enough to be almost hidden within the profile of the building itself.

OPPOSITE, TOP LEFT

Angled ceilings, walls and lots of light make the small kitchen-dining area feel bigger than it is. A small balcony is reached through the glazed door to the rear of this space.

TOP RIGHT

A line of slot windows and a fixed high level window at the apex of the cathedral ceiling wrap the living area in light.

BOTTOM

Tucked below the slanting roof and bounded by the balustrade of the adjacent staircase the kitchen is a masterpiece of tight planning.

Nothing could even begin to compete with the sheer mischief and whimsicality of that shaggy windblown roof

All in all, the interiors are as simple as the exterior is complex. But possibly that's because nothing could even begin to compete with the sheer mischief and whimsicality of that shaggy windblown roof. Raphael feels it is a structure that fulfils his needs in many different ways. 'I wanted something sensitive, but different. Something that worked for me as a Melbourne bolthole, but also contributed something new and exciting to the neighbourhood. I also wanted it to reflect the philosophy by which I now live my life – you could call it something like 'all you need is less'.'

Design Notes

/ Weathered steel planter boxes filled with hardy native grasses clad the upper level. These fulfil the environmental requirements for permeability and open space, while providing substantial insulation to the building itself.

/ Progressively recessing the profile of the outer corners on the upper level delivers a dramatic silhouette while simultaneously preventing overshadowing of the public spaces.

/ Oversize intersecting slot windows on the upper storey create their own design statement. A skylight above the stairwell introduces verticality into the small interior and allows light penetration into the depths of the lower storey.

OPPOSITE, TOP LEFT
The small dining area alongside the kitchen is lit from four directions. Although out of shot in this picture, a skylight throws another angle of light into the space below.

TOP RIGHT
A slot skylight window above the bed allows this small interior space to feel anything but claustrophobic.

BOTTOM
The depth of colour of the window joinery against the white walls acts to frame views of the neighbourhood beyond.

OVER PAGE
Shaggy greenery climbing the walls against the blue of a winter sky is an arresting sight on an inner-city corner.

Grass House

78M²

Fitzroy, Melbourne, VIC
David Luck Architect

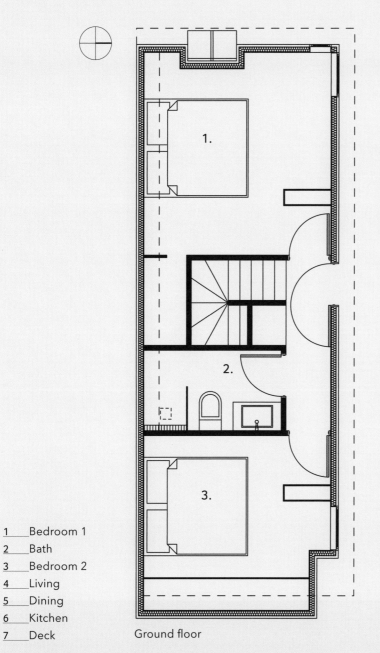

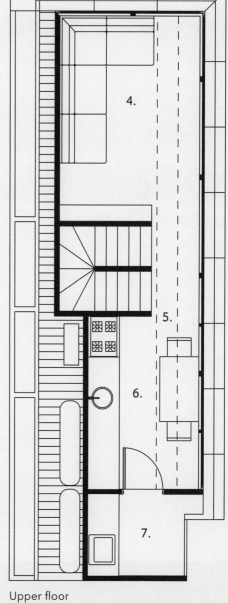

1 ____ Bedroom 1
2 ____ Bath
3 ____ Bedroom 2
4 ____ Living
5 ____ Dining
6 ____ Kitchen
7 ____ Deck

Ground floor   Upper floor

Annandale Guesthouse

58M²

Annandale, Sydney, NSW

Day Bukh Architects

Photography by
Katherine Lu

173

'A bonus for the client' is how Matt Day from architectural practice Day Bukh describes the green credentials of much of what they design. 'As a practice we are deeply interested in designing ecological and sustainable buildings for the Australian context. If the design, and its particular context, is thought through right from the beginning, then stuff like solar gain can be used for free.'

David Ginges and Bronwen Booth's achingly pretty garden guesthouse benefitted from this commitment. By embedding strategies that harness or control the power of the sun, Day has produced an object of beauty that also has a 7.5 Star Energy Rating.

Although a mere 58m², a surprising sense of space, both internal and external, belies the structure's humble dimensions. This is achieved by combining devices which reflect the architects' interests in both Scandinavian modernism and Japanese minimalism. The most obvious of these is the pagoda-like structure of the roof and the way it interacts with the front facade. Deeply-recessed clerestory windows form a light-filled trough between the wide eaves above and the secondary roof below, giving the effect of two roofs. The upper one seems to float, unsupported except by light. Glazing the windows in an opaque glass similar in tone to the painted walls below enhances the illusion.

Playing tricks with perspective and space does not end here. Once inside, the space below these deep eaves seems to have disappeared, as the interior walls continue down on the same vertical plane as the clerestory glazing above it. Almost concealed in this 'lost' area, however, is a streamlined wall of storage that allows the exposed footprint to be fully habitable, sleek and clutter-free. Booth loves the fact that the small interior can be kept visually spare. '[There is] heaps of storage you can't see. You don't need to add anything so furniture doesn't clutter up the space.'

PREVIOUS PAGE
A swimming pool and lush plantings separate the main house from the guesthouse, giving privacy to both; light glowing through the clerestory windows of the guesthouse appears to make its roof float in space.

OPPOSITE
The colour similarity between the oiled timber joinery and the timber floors functions to connect the horizontal and vertical planes while also imbuing a note of luxury.

174

We are deeply interested in designing ecological and sustainable buildings for the Australian context

OPPOSITE, TOP
Exposed roof trusses and architraves, also in oiled timber, are a visually dominant element throughout. Locating the kitchen (and bathroom out of shot) centrally between the living and bedroom areas provides sound separation between the two.

BOTTOM
The bedroom has its own private deck, and is kept clutter-free by the provision of ample storage in the recessed space below the clerestory windows. Because the doors to this storage area appear as though on the same vertical plane as the wall that contains the windows above, they do not intrude on the small footprint.

The structure was designed with the possibility of becoming the owners' full-time home in the future. Sound separation between sleeping and living areas was considered essential. Consequently, unlike the usual open-plan living room and kitchen, a small kitchen situated within the depth of the storage wall separates the spaces for living and sleeping. Across the connecting passageway that is also the movement area for the kitchen is the utility area and bathroom. Despite the small size, their tight design means they operate efficiently while providing the necessary buffer from the noise of the TV.

Privacy from the main dwelling is also not an issue. Separate entrances were the key and Day gave thoughtful consideration as to how to control interaction between the two buildings. Staggering the living areas of both so that they had no direct visual connection was the solution and focusing the outlook of the guesthouse towards the side further improved the outcome. Fencing and greenery along the outer edges of the adjacent deck direct the view away from the main house while increasing the impression of space from within.

Interiors are painted white and the exterior a soft grey. The warm tones of oiled cedar used both inside and out connect the spaces and add a note of sensuality to an otherwise unadorned material palette. The modernist-inspired window joinery and exposed roof trusses define the interiors, and bargeboards and jointers in the same material add complexity to the fibre cement board clad exterior.

By cleverly combining light and volume with a simple palette of natural materials Day has produced an interior that, while pleasantly lit, is never glaring or hot in summer, and requires only a minimum of heating in winter. Deep eaves protect the interior from excess heat during summer, while double glazing prevents excess heat loss during the cooler months. Passive strategies like this are only part of the equation, and active techniques are employed as well. LED lighting, energy- and water-saving devices, rainwater collection and sustainably sourced and renewable building materials, all contribute to a 7.5 Star Energy Rating.

Planning regulations in NSW allow 'complying developments' such as this comfortable and elegant secondary dwelling as a matter of course, with the proviso that they add 'amenity' to their site and environs. Booth believes it has produced far more for its owners than this. As a means to sustainable living as they 'age in place', its value is certainly immense in a practical sense, but in terms of pleasure just one word suffices. 'Luxurious!'

Design Notes

/ Concealed storage within 'functional' walls allow the use of a minimum of furniture, with the result that small spaces appear spacious and uncluttered.

/ Deep eaves are among many of the passive and active design strategies employed by the architect.

/ The material palette is simple yet not basic. Oiled timber for joinery and external decorative trim is not the cheapest option but its contribution to both the environmental and aesthetic requirements justified its use.

OPPOSITE, TOP
Wrapping the outer corner of the living room in a combination of sliding and bi-fold doors enhances its feeling of spaciousness.

BOTTOM
A small dining space alongside the kitchen is a peaceful spot to start the day.

OVER PAGE
The living room has everything needed for relaxation. A raised ceiling above the seating area defines the space intended for seating.

Annandale Guesthouse

<u>58M²</u>
Annandale, Sydney, NSW
Day Bukh Architects

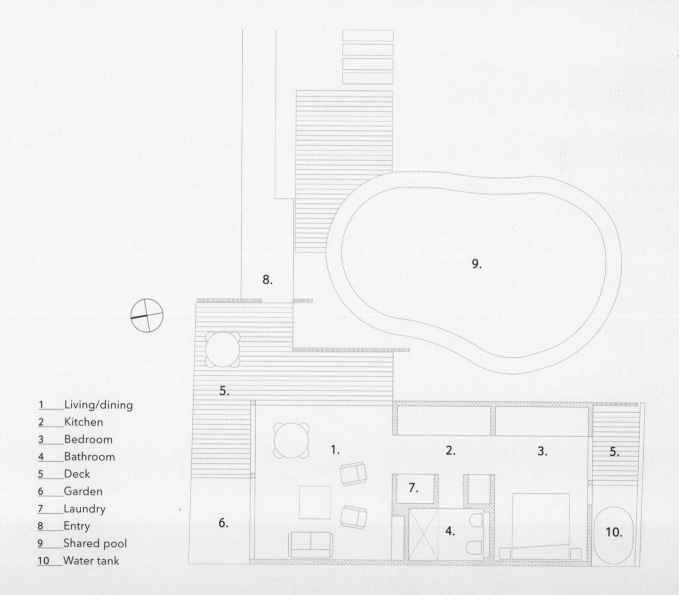

<u>1</u>   Living/dining
<u>2</u>   Kitchen
<u>3</u>   Bedroom
<u>4</u>   Bathroom
<u>5</u>   Deck
<u>6</u>   Garden
<u>7</u>   Laundry
<u>8</u>   Entry
<u>9</u>   Shared pool
<u>10</u>   Water tank

Foster House

/ **68M²**

South Gippsland, VIC

Allison Hopper Architect

Photography by
Daniel Dixon

Award

Houses Awards 2015: New
House under 200m² Shortlist

In the rolling countryside of South Gippsland, close to where
Wilsons Promontory juts into the Southern Ocean, lies a small
perfect weekender. Situated within the shelter of encircling pines
and blackwoods, with long grasses sighing in the wind, it is as far
from the rush of urban life as can be imagined.

No deep porches, no allusions to local agricultural
architecture, not even a repurposed rural cottage, the crisp cube
is more typical of urban environments than the standard rural
retreat. It represents 'critical regionalism' – a school of thought
that sees landscape, climate, light and geographical form as
architecture in its purest form.

Nonetheless, Allison Hopper, the architect and co-owner, does
not see the design as incongruent with its rural setting. 'The design
was inspired by the natural beauty of the blackwood trees and by
the topography, the grandeur of the rolling hills within and beyond
the site. We saw it a simple sculptural form set in a natural setting
– an object on the landscape rather than of it – one that uses visual
contrast to amplify the power and beauty of its setting.'

In part, Hopper was bound by what had gone before. A
previous owner had erected, but not completed, a 6m² by 6m² two-
storey structure on 'the best building-platform on the site.' The steel
frame of this had become twisted, but was judged to be structurally
sound enough to act as the basis for what Hopper had in mind.
'After camping on the site for most of a year and experiencing the
way light, wind and rain moved across it, we decided to make use
of what we had. We also enjoyed the close views across the dam
at the foot of the embankment it stood on, and the distant views of
Corner Inlet to the east.'

PREVIOUS PAGE
Light from the translucent
polycarbonate stairwell window
lends the building the appearance
of a Chinese lantern.

OPPOSITE
Repetition of the detailing and
placement of window and doors
gives the small building cohesion.

After camping on the site for most of a year and experiencing the way light, wind and rain moved across it, we decided to make use of what we had

OPPOSITE, TOP LEFT

Unlike in most holiday homes where outdoor flow is the form, exit points are deliberately controlled with railings across the sliding doors. This forces the viewer to observe nature from within the building instead of allowing the two to blend.

TOP RIGHT

A discreetly located single door is the only entry point to the house.

BOTTOM

Windows onto the double-height void above the dining area flood this area with light at all times of the day.

Large enough to accommodate family and friends as well as the owners themselves, the pre-existing frame was ideally sized for an intimately scaled weekend retreat. Its retention saved money as well. 'It was never going to be huge, but we could see that by placing the spaces carefully we could form a bright and spacious whole – roomy enough for all to relax and enjoy the natural world in surroundings that would feel simple and uncluttered.'

Strategically-placed windows and large glazed doors allowed sightlines and light to penetrate across the structure to the other side, maximising the impression of space within the interior. Unusually, replicating the steel balustrade across the large first floor sliding doors on the level below prevents the more common indoor-outdoor connection to the outdoors. Hopper explains that, although not usual 'it was a deliberate ploy. Controlling the points of exit brings attention to how, in an environment like this, the connection between the inside and outside is always permeable. It's very different to how we are forced to live in the city.'

The floorplan is simple. With no walls, except those around the utility core in one corner, the ground floor is given over to a series of interconnected living, eating and cooking areas. A double-height void above the dining area, and translucent polycarbonate cladding of the adjacent stairwell, floods it with light and once again encourages modest dimensions to appear more generous than they are.

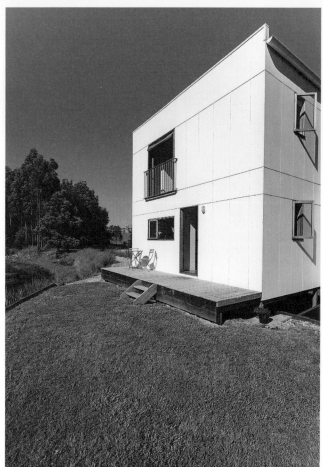

The upper level is occupied by two bedrooms. Lit from both sides and accessed from the landing alongside the void, they too are deceptively spacious. As in the living area below, their colour and material palette is deliberately muted. Walls are white and the floors recycled blackbutt; the natural honey tones of the birch plywood lining the inner wall of the stairwell is the only burst of colour. Each of these was a deliberate choice. Hopper sees simplicity like this as a respite from 'the chaotic, full colour palette of the city. This is a space kept deliberately uncomplicated – both visually and spatially – in contrast with the complexity of city life where so much more is needed, and provided.'

Modest though it is, this building is far more than a mere container for shelter. It is a structure with a heart and soul, the sort of retreat where memories are made.

Design Notes

/ The severity of the 6m cube form is leavened by the double-height polycarbonate panel alongside the spiral staircase. Being translucent, this glows at night like a Chinese lantern, and during the day diffuses the somewhat harsh northerly light.

/ Windows and doors have been deliberately positioned so that clear sightlines pierce the structure from side to side.

/ Suspended on steel posts 600mm off the ground, air moves as easily under it as it does around and above.

OPPOSITE, TOP LEFT
The circular staircase, although functional and strikingly decorative, was chosen because it could be erected onsite without the help of tradesmen.

TOP RIGHT
Most of the furniture is mid-century modern in style as the small neat dimensions do not overwhelm the modest size of the rooms.

BOTTOM RIGHT
A shell and gravel pathway appears to lead only to the non-opening lightbox of the stairwell but in fact slips neatly around the foot of the building to access the entrance deck to the rear.

BOTTOM LEFT
Understanding of the complexity of this small building is gained from looking down from the landing alongside the bedrooms.

OVER PAGE
The romance of the Milky Way reflecting in the dark waters of the dam below the house is but one of the reasons for locating this holiday home deep in undisturbed countryside.

Foster House

<u>68M²</u>
South Gippsland, VIC
Allison Hopper Architect

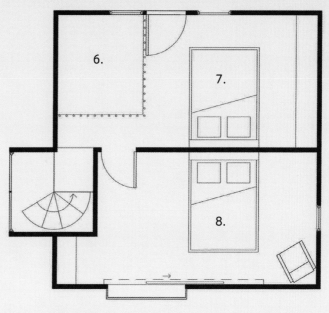

Upper floor

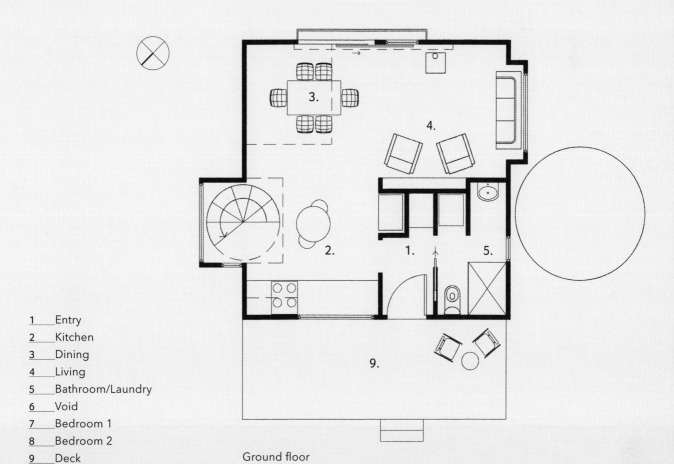

Ground floor

<u>1</u>	Entry
<u>2</u>	Kitchen
<u>3</u>	Dining
<u>4</u>	Living
<u>5</u>	Bathroom/Laundry
<u>6</u>	Void
<u>7</u>	Bedroom 1
<u>8</u>	Bedroom 2
<u>9</u>	Deck

Premaydena House

80M² + DECKS

Premaydena Valley, TAS

Misho + Associates

Photography by
Peter Whyte

Awards
2015 World Architectural
Festival Singapore –
Residential Category.
Shortlisted

'Boxes within and beside each other' is how architect Misho Vasiljevich describes the eyecatching building that's drawing attention to the Premaydena valley of south-eastern Tasmania. Rather than beating a modest retreat into its landscape, here is a building - uncomplicatedly modular in construction - that positively shouts 'Here I am! Look at me! Think about me!'

Wrapping the external perimeter are sliding metal screens, starkly coloured in the same fiery reds and oranges of lichen on the rocks of local beaches and spring flowering Tasmanian waratah. Unbroken by windows, and with only slight variations in colour indicating the entry points, enclosure such as this is a bold statement indeed. Views are typically of paramount importance for holiday homes, but these screens appear to direct the gaze away from the very reason for the structure's existence. Vasiljevich is unapologetic. 'There are practical considerations - security, protection from the north-easterly, overheating from the west, bushfire - but [because they can be opened in any arrangement] they don't define how the views should be interacted with. It's more a case of where you are and what you're doing … sitting on the north side with a good book, or chatting with friends on the west.'

Just as these external screens recall the architecture of the Japanese teahouse, so too does the enclosed interior structure - what its architect describes as 'its soft centre.' Its form is soothingly uncomplicated. Based on the grid associated with the traditional *tsubo* measurement still in use in Japan today, it functions as a series of interconnected modules, side by side and within each other. Daily living, eating and cooking takes place in a single 6 x 6m cube. The bedrooms make use of two-thirds of another, while the wet area, the remaining one-third, is itself divided into two bathrooms and a laundry.

PREVIOUS PAGE
Brightly painted metal screens, deliberately designed to resemble sliding shoji screen doors, can be fully closed to protect all glazed areas when the house is unoccupied.

OPPOSITE
Shallow steps leading to wraparound decks are all the timber that is exposed when the house is secured behind its protective screens. Bushfire is a threat to be taken seriously in areas where close access to water is not guaranteed.

194

Just as these external screens recall the architecture of the Japanese teahouse, so too does the enclosed interior structure

The Japanese aesthetic is not limited to these pleasing, harmonious rhythms. Shoji-like insect screens retract into walls, the central partings of glazed sliding doors align with opened external panels, beds centre on openings, and interior finishing is deliberately minimal. Nothing is allowed to disturb the essential impression of tranquillity.

Similarly, the exteriors of this inner core are unadorned. Although glazed in large sections with externally-hung sliding doors, what walls exist are clad in rough-sawn grooved plywood, stained a softer shade of the orange of the external screens. Just as the external frame – prefabricated steel erected onsite in a day – was designed to minimise the costs associated with building in a remote location, so too were the modules that form the core structure. Although the associated joinery elements were made from hardwood harvested and milled in a nearby valley, all were constructed in a factory in Launceston and assembled onsite.

A wide clerestory window facing south bathes the interior with a soft, cool light when the shutters are closed and offers the perfect place through which to watch the resident population of eagles riding the thermals that rise above the escarpment to the rear. This is what Vasiljevich describes as 'the micro view. The valley below, the bay out in the distance, they're the macro, but right here looking through the clerestory watching the eagles against the scudding clouds – there's something very magical.'

Owners, David Burns and Tania Soghomonian, come to this special spot to unwind. Whether it's the vista of valleys unfolding below, or eagles riding the thermals above their heads, it's as far from what Burns describes as 'the circus of cars, buildings and work' as can be imagined.

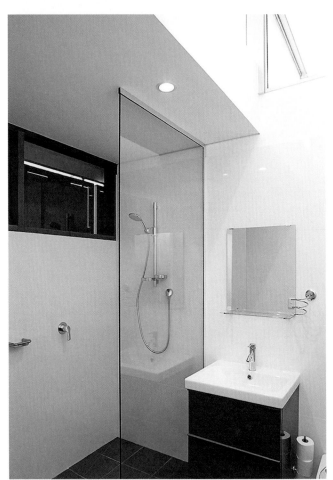

Design Notes

/ Brightly painted metal screens form an external enclosure around the living areas within. The colours reference orange lichen abundant on rocks at nearby beaches and the red flowers of the Tasmanian waratah – while also providing security and protection from bush fire.

/ The cuboid form of the internal living core contains a series of smaller 'boxes', the dimensions of which are based on the traditional Japanese *tsubo* measurement. This device enables maximum efficiency in the tight floorplan while simultaneously referencing the design aesthetic underpinning the project as a whole.

/ Labour and transport costs were controlled by constructing in modular form. All elements were prefabricated, then disassembled and reassembled after transportation to site. The epoxy paint-finished steel frame took only one day to assemble.

OPPOSITE, TOP LEFT
A south facing clerestory window is the perfect place through which to watch the resident eagle population riding the thermals from the escarpment behind.

TOP RIGHT
Both bedrooms have an ensuite bathroom and these, plus the laundry, form part of the service core in the heart of the building.

BOTTOM
When fully closed, the painted screens create a 'box' to be unwrapped. Their colours were inspired by the orange lichen found on local beaches and the fiery red of the spring flowering Tasmanian waratah.

OVER PAGE
Eucalypt and dry grasses are icons of Australian landscape, and the surroundings have been left deliberately undomesticated.

Premaydena House

<u>80M² + DECKS</u>
Premaydena Valley, TAS
Misho + Associates

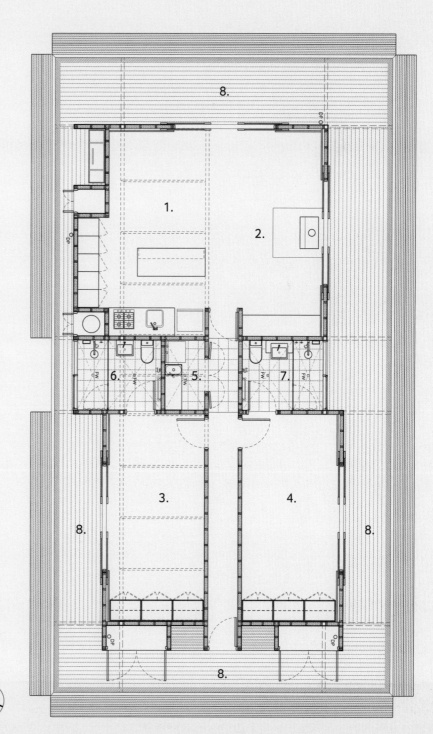

1____Kitchen/Dining
2____Living
3____Bedroom 1
4____Bedroom 2
5____Laundry
6____Ensuite 1
7____Ensuite 2
8____Deck

MIELBRE

Lincoln House

80M² + 25M² COVERED DECKS

Samford Valley, Brisbane, QLD

BAAhouse

Photography by
Carole Margand

Once scorned, the humble granny flat is undergoing a twenty-first century rehabilitation. The new order has brought with it a range of new names. Now just as likely to be called a studio, a pod, a retreat or a pavilion, the function of most is still to provide additional living space. These days, granny is as often as not living in the main house while the secondary dwelling is reserved for younger family members, or even tenants.

Not so Neil and Patricia Fitzpatrick's house in the Samford Valley area of Brisbane. It truly is a granny – and granddad – flat. Tired of the upkeep of their big house, and with the family grown and gone, the Fitzpatricks no longer needed its rambling spaces. However, their daughter did. What Patricia describes as a 'time-of-life change' was the obvious solution. They would build a granny flat in the grounds and live at the bottom of the garden.

Thus far, the story deviates only a slightly from the traditional narrative. But tradition is turned on its head by the architectural ambition and sophistication of the Fitzpatricks' new home. They wanted a home to celebrate their love of fine design as well as provide comfortable, easy-care accommodation well into their old age.

Already admirers of the work of local architectural practice BAAhouse, they commissioned the practice to design what architect Claus Ejlertsen describes as 'yes … a granny flat, but one with a whole lot more going for it'.

The design is not a complex one. As much as anything, it is the easily read nature of it that gives this dwelling its appeal. Formed from a series of variously-sized interconnecting cubes which fluidly advance and retreat under a single overarching skillion roof, and animated by a recurring motif of vertical posts and battens, it is elevated to poetry by the sheer grace of its light-footed attachment to the land beneath. Lifting the structure on a cat's cradle of galvanised posts may have been a strategy to reduce foundation costs and to protect against termite invasion, but the result is far more. Near water it would bring a wading bird to mind, but in the green reaches of Brisbane's western suburbs, it hovers like a treehouse within the branches of its jacaranda. In time, it will sit grounded by plantings but in the short term, it is happy just to float.

PREVIOUS PAGE
A single skillion roof that over-sails both house and decks produces the impression of a large and imposing house.

OPPOSITE
Sheltered, but not enclosed, decks are not included in the dimensions of a secondary dwelling in Queensland, yet add immensely to the usability of a small house in a climate that allows outdoor living eight months of the year.

204

What Patricia describes as a 'time-of-life change' was the obvious solution. They would build a granny flat in the grounds and live at the bottom of the garden

Verticality is the theme which ties the exterior together. In addition to the leggy foundations, charcoal posts support the roof, vertically mounted grooved cement board clads the structure and slatted privacy screens separate the decks. Battens made from New Guinea rosewood add interest and visually link to the protruding roof beams that punctuate the horizontal planes of the soffits.

Site restrictions stipulated that the structure to face due west, an orientation which required a strategy to control overheating for much of the year. Ejlertsen's solution was to wrap the westerly facades with deep covered decks which extend the living spaces and operate as a cooling zone for the house to their rear. 'Without these, and the huge amount of insulation in their ceiling spaces, the interior would cook like an egg. The polycarbonate clerestory windows below the roof perimeter also keeps sun off the glass at the end of day when it's still very hot.' Fortunately, local regulations do not count decks as part of the footprint, despite them adding significantly to the living area.

Sheltering the interior was only one of the strategies for heat control. Ceiling fans on 3.6m high ceilings and banks of louvre windows provide year-round cross-ventilation. As a result, air conditioning is needed only in the hottest months.

The interior's finishes are simple yet polished, and the restrained palette displays its blend of serviceable yet elegant elements to good effect. The tawny hues of spotted gum, used on both floors and decking, extends to wrap the kitchen island unit. Charcoal cabinetry draws attention to the recurring vertical elements provided by the glazing while white walls and ceilings offer an unobtrusive background for the owners' possessions.

A home office provides sound-separation between the living area and the main bedroom, and a second bedroom tucks away to the rear of this.

The owners are quietly happy with their new home. They describe it as 'relaxing'. Their family in the old house up the garden thinks it's pretty cool too. They're wondering how they can make the old house work as well as the granny flat in the garden. Now there's a turn-up for the books!

Design Notes

/ The building takes the form of a series of interconnecting boxes under a single skillion roof.

/ Raising the structure on galvanised metal stilts protects against termites and adds to cooling during the hottest months of the year.

/ Westerly facades are protected from excess heat and thunderstorms by deep covered porches.

OPPOSITE, TOP
The louvre windows in the home office are an example of the recurrent use of horizontal lines to thematically link different areas. Positioning the office between the bedrooms and living areas provides necessary sound separation.

BOTTOM
A recessed bank of storage – both open and concealed – means only what is wanted stays visible.

OVER PAGE
Louvre windows and a ceiling fan in the bedroom mean mechanical air-conditioning can be used as a last resort, even on the steamiest of summer nights.

Lincoln House

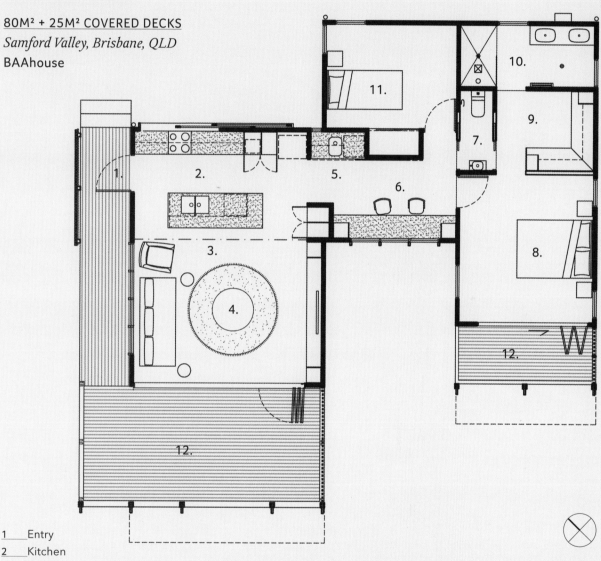

80M² + 25M² COVERED DECKS
Samford Valley, Brisbane, QLD
BAAhouse

1   Entry
2   Kitchen
3   Dining
4   Lounge
5   Laundry
6   Study
7   WC
8   Main bedroom
9   WIR
10   Ensuite/Bathroom
11   Bedroom 2
12   Deck

Florence St House

80M²

Coburg, Melbourne, VIC

Nest Architects

Photography by
Nic Granleese

In 2011 a fortuitous dip in Melbourne's runaway housing market presented architect Emilio Fuscaldo and partner Anna Krien with the opportunity to indulge what Fuscaldo describes as his 'old-world desire to own a patch of land'. Perhaps it was his Italian heritage – it could also be the desire of every young architect to build their own home – but for Fuscaldo owning a patch of dirt and a sunny outlook was infinitely preferable to forever belonging to 'generation rent'.

The 160m² backyard site was certainly compact, but it was situated in fast-emerging Coburg, close to family and workplaces, and with its own access off the rear laneway, the surroundings were private and leafy. It was also north-facing, with the boundary running along this facade cushioned by the permanent presence of the laneway. With a site of this size this extension of outlook was important. Although the immediate surroundings would necessarily be constrained by the tightness of the site, the outlook would remain open – a factor to consider when building in areas where future intensive development is envisaged.

With a commitment to sustainable design also a factor in determining Fuscaldo's plans for the site, this north-facing orientation was ideal. 'Anna and I are committed to the ideal of environmentally conscious living and I was determined to mesh architectural practices that support this with our desire to create a lovely family home. But we were adamant that the result should not be gained at the the price of sacrificing aesthetic sensibilities. Our home had to reflect what we are.'

It also had to be practical and, since completion in 2012, two children have joined Fuscaldo and Krien. At 80m² the footprint is tight for four people but with every square millimetre, both inside and out, considered and effective, it remains a comfortable family home. Despite the tight site, Fuscaldo was determined not to relinquish his desire for a veggie garden and by installing a 'living' roof – a 200mm blanket of soil and vegetation instead of the more conventional tiles or tin – made use of what is often wasted space while simultaneously insulating the structure below.

All windows and doors are double glazed, and the passive heating achieved through exposing the polished concrete slab minimises the need for the ancillary heating embedded in its core. The walls might appear to be old school heat-leaking single brick, but in fact all are double-skinned. The cavities between two 'skins' provide space for generous insulation.

PREVIOUS PAGE
A roof-top garden in inner-city suburbia fulfils the owner's need to keep his hands in the soil. It also is a good source of insulation to the house below and addresses the issues around permeability (how much land can be built over with an impermeable structure) on a small site.

OPPOSITE
A double skinned wall of recycled bricks was one of the ways inexpensive materials were used to good effect; another is the use of Formply as a dramatic ceiling material – being ready finished this did not need extra trade time to plaster or paint it.

214

By installing a 'living' roof – a 200mm blanket of soil and vegetation – Fuscaldo made use of what is often wasted space while simultaneously insulating the structure below

OPPOSITE, TOP LEFT
Repurposed industrial furniture
has been given a new lease of life
in the kitchen.

TOP RIGHT
The careful placing of everyday
objects on open shelving allows
them to be as much decorative as
functional.

BOTTOM RIGHT
An asymmetric pergola that
extends on the same plane as the
roof behind it adds a touch of
whimsy, but also serves to deflect
sun from the interior.

BOTTOM LEFT
The transparency of clerestory
windows above the heft of brick
walls is a pleasing contrast.

PAGE 216
Oiled cedar for the exterior joinery
was a deliberately organic choice
of material.

PAGE 217
Using recycled and repurposed
materials and furnishings
both stretched the budget and
minimised environmental waste
throughout the building process.

The benefits of building with such heavyweight materials, thereby achieving what is termed as high thermal mass, are many. Melbourne's climate is prone to extremes, with some summer temperatures being as uncomfortable as those in the depths of winter. Fuscaldo recounts how '… completely unscientifically, we did an analysis that showed we had a consistent summer temperature of 20-23° which is about 4-6° cooler than outside. Obviously, minimising the need for heating in winter is good, but keeping temperatures stable throughout the year is a really pleasant benefit from building in this way.'

Many of the building materials are recycled – a deliberate strategy that contributes in a major way to the appearance of the finished result. A small budget played a part in this, but rather than being a hindrance Fuscaldo perceived it '… as more a way to open up other opportunities'. Defining elements such as the secondhand red brick walls were left exposed and plumbing runs defiantly visible. 'It is very much about honouring both the building process and the materials. We didn't want to buy a cheap new tap that pretended to be an expensive new tap; rather we chose good quality recycled materials and repurposed them to work for us.'

Unlike conventionally installed kitchens which invariably aim to conceal their raison d'etre behind built-in cabinetry, Fuscaldo and Krien's is completely freestanding. Carefully chosen secondhand items provide functionality without compromising the air of casual competence found in any workshop. What was once a workbench in a joinery shop now houses the sink and food preparation area, while the careful arrangement of items on the open shelves above is as much a decorative element as mere storage.

Leaving the heavy duty building materials exposed, along with the utilitarianism of the fit-out, risked making the vibe spartan rather than homely. The effect is anything but, and a lighthearted eclectic atmosphere that is part funky urban and part serious eco-thoughtfulness is the dominant impression. Fuscaldo admits that as the children grow it mightn't continue to be the ideal home it presently is, but for now he is content. 'We have created a home that's a real reflection of who we are. We don't feel that has been compromised in any way. We are realistic about what it gives us and what the future might bring. But for the moment it realises everything we set out to achieve.'

Design Notes

/ Vegetation-covered 'living' roof is both a design feature and one of several elements that contribute to the eco-credentials of the structure.

/ Direct access and a wider outlook is possible due to the position of the original laneway on the northern boundary.

/ Deliberately using recycled building materials and fittings made the budget go further while generating a warmly eclectic design aesthetic.

OPPOSITE, TOP LEFT
The height of the ceiling gives the comparatively small living area an unexpectedly generous feeling. Running windows all the way up to the ceiling captures light throughout the year.

TOP RIGHT
The master bedroom is a quiet and private space on the corner furthest away from the laneway.

BOTTOM
The patina of use on both materials and furnishings adds textural interest and makes the living area a warm and inviting space.

OVER PAGE
The grassy lawn on the roof of the house is a peaceful place to observe the neighbourhood at dusk.

Florence St House

<u>80M²</u>
Coburg, Melbourne, VIC
Nest Architects

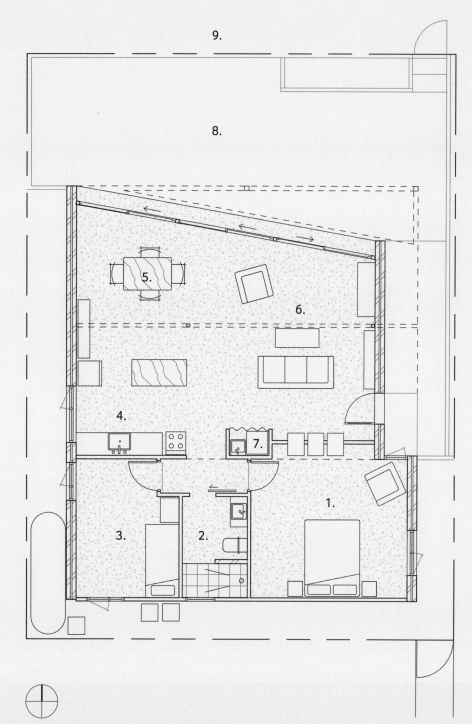

1 ___ Bed
2 ___ Bathroom
3 ___ Bathroom 2
4 ___ Kitchen
5 ___ Dining
6 ___ Living
7 ___ Laundry
8 ___ Yard
9 ___ Laneway

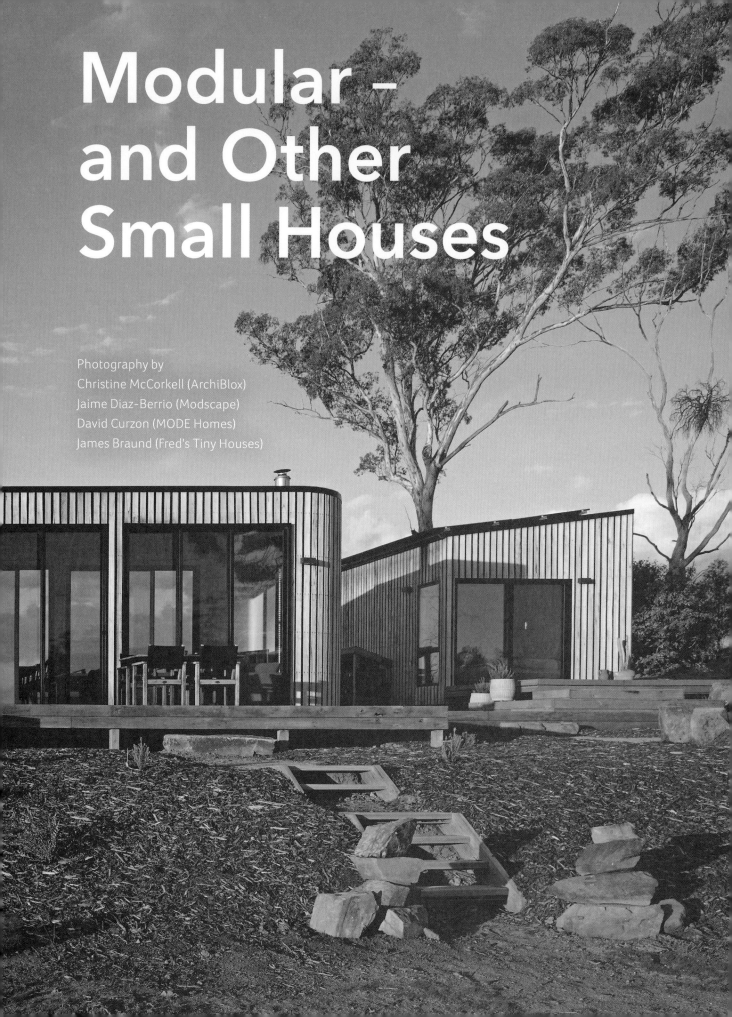

Modular – and Other Small Houses

Photography by
Christine McCorkell (ArchiBlox)
Jaime Diaz-Berrio (Modscape)
David Curzon (MODE Homes)
James Braund (Fred's Tiny Houses)

Custom designed and built housing is the norm in Australia, and all except one of the examples in this book are versions of this. For decades, however, the construction industry has attempted to capitalise on the savings made by using prefabricated elements under controlled conditions. All too often the results are cheaply constructed, over-simplified structures lacking any architectural merit. It does not have to be this way.

The best contemporary modular homes (the term replaces the negatively perceived 'prefab') are aesthetically sophisticated, highly 'specced' and hugely insulated, and it is architects as much as volume builders who are producing design-dense, high quality versions to meet an ever-expanding market. Often designed with highly adaptable components to meet the requirements of specific briefs, factory built modular homes are second rate no longer. Those mentioned here (a tiny selection of what is available) are small, and in some cases, single module versions of what are often infinitely modifiable systems.

ArchiBlox

Architect Bill McCorkell of Victorian-based firm ArchiBlox sees modular construction as 'an amazing opportunity to make the best use of off-site procurement'. Using modular set designs and elements, each commission is configured to meet the individual needs of the client, the budget and the site. 'Building under controlled conditions allows the best use of materials and time, with consequent savings passed on to the client. We design big, rather than build big.' All designs are fully modifiable and through focusing on passive solar and sustainable design principles, Archiblox's modular homes reach an 8 Star Energy Rating.

The example on the previous page is a full-time home rather than a weekender. The owners moved in just seven days after the house had been connected to its waiting foundations and services.

WWW.ARCHIBLOX.COM.AU

PREVIOUS PAGE
Wraparound vertical cladding and over-height windows and doors give this ArchiBlox building an imposing presence. The whimsical curving of an outer corner adds further interest.

OPPOSITE, TOP
The Modscape cabin's crisp form and outsized windows denote an architectural heritage that contrasts with the deliberate rusticity of an outer shell of reused corrugated iron.

BOTTOM
Constructed in such a way that it can be flat-packed for transportation and unfolded in a matter of hours onto waiting foundations, this MODE home is as comfortable and solid as many twice its size.

Modscape

Modscape designs and constructs prefabricated modular buildings with structural steel frames infilled with pre-formed highly insulated Structural Insulated Panels (SIP). This construction board is made from sandwiching a thick layer of insulation between internal and external cladding, and result is cheap to run and inexpensive to maintain. Modscape's designs are fully customisable, with a variety of module sizes allowing extreme flexibility of size and design.

The 65m² single module cabin illustrated on page 224 (top) serves as a secure and homely retreat for its overseas-based owner. The client worked with Modscape's team of in-house architects and designers to create a completely off-grid retreat. With a decorative secondary cladding of recycled corrugated iron over a watertight core, it is disguised as a modest agricultural building – similar in form and appearance to those that dot the surrounding countryside. Beneath its rustic exterior, however, is a crisply modern home with all modern amenities. The 35m² of decking expands the living space.

WWW.MODSCAPE.COM.AU

MODE Homes

Mode Homes' architect and owner, Matthew Dynon, looked for efficiencies in transporting the completed structure. 'Moving anything larger than 3.5m wide and 4.6m high is considerably more expensive than something smaller. You need a pilot vehicle, permissions to raise power lines for example. We've devised what we called construction, where the building is largely constructed in our premises under controlled conditions, and then 'folded' using our own hinge system to produce what is in effect a 'flatpack' structure. The result is that a standard 80m² structure can be transported to site on a single truck, in a package 3.2m high and 3.5m wide. Keeping loads to this size means not only are long distance transportation costs very affordable, but it also means modular building is possible where access for a full-sized modular building to be lifted or manoeuvred into place isn't possible.'

It's also very quick, as once the foundations are in place, the building can be 'unfolded' by two people in half a day, minimising the problems which come with uncertain weather, or lack of local skilled labour. Only minor finishing details such as capping on parapets and internal connections to services need to be added. See page 224 (bottom) for an example.

WWW.MODEHOMES.COM.AU

Container Homes

The ultimate in box living has to be a converted shipping container. Slightly cheaper to build than conventional buildings, container homes are 'modular' only in so far as they are formed from combinations of modules sized originally for economical transportation. Their robust structural properties mean that they are relatively easy to modify into homes of different sizes and configurations, although insulating to the required amount, and weather sealing the openings, are expensive and necessary parts of the process.

As extra width and length can be achieved through welding more than one together along the edges of reinforced openings cut in the walls, or extra storeys by stacking vertically, almost any shaped structure is possible, as long as the building block look is to your taste. External decorative cladding can be overlaid however if the industrial appearance is too confronting, and decks and pergolas attached to soften the look and add amenity.

The most frequently used are two sizes that are still commonly referred to as 20 and 40 foot containers. (This equates to an interior footprint of approximately 13.5m² and 28m² respectively). The most successful for accommodation are the High Cube models because the 2.7m height allows for the roof to be heavily insulated without forgoing a workable 2.4m ceiling height. Less common than those with a 2.4m height, these are however harder to source secondhand and more expensive.

In recent years, specialist companies have sprung up across Australia, and every state has suppliers who will supply a variety of styles. To reduce the costs involved in transportation it is best to look for one local to where you intend to build. For inspiration and contacts see the site below.

WWW. SHIPPINGCONTAINERHOMESAUSTRALIA.COM.AU

228

Tiny Houses

Originating in North America about a decade ago, and now growing in popularity in Australia, the 'Tiny House' movement and the anti-consumerist ideology behind it is very different from the small houses featured in this book. For a start, they are quite literally tiny, with an internal area no greater than 16m². They are also nominally mobile, being built on a roadworthy trailer of those dimensions. The reality is many never move from the site on which they are constructed, because unlike caravans and trailer homes, tiny homes are sturdily built with permanent building materials, and it is this consequent weight that makes them unsuitable for frequent relocation. Although the per metre build cost can be high, their diminutive size makes them cheap to build. Semi-constructed or fully outfitted versions are available via specialist builders (see example opposite). Very different to modular homes, tiny houses are legally classified as mobile homes (in the same category as caravans) and, as such, avoid many of the regulations around permanent construction.

While anti-consumerism partly accounts for their emergence, the growing unaffordability of the land on which to site a permanent home is undoubtedly the main reason. Not all states or regions are tiny house-friendly so finding a site is the first obstacle. How the structure will interact with the necessary utilities is another important consideration. Will it be completely self sufficient in terms of waste disposal, water and electricity generation, or will it be linked in some way to locally provided services? If the latter, how will these be paid for?

Fred Schultz of Victoria-based Fred's Tiny Houses aims to educate prospective tiny homers as much as build Australian specific versions which are 'strong durable and homey'. Workshops run from his Castlemaine premises cover topics such as explaining the complex regulatory environment around the siting of tiny houses in Victoria and NSW, to illustrating the reality of living off-grid through tours of his own home.

WWW.FREDSTINYHOUSES.COM.AU

OPPOSITE
Tiny houses usually feature ingenious ways to save space with multi-function built-in furniture.

Perhaps on coming to the end of this book you ask yourself – is this for me? Could I live in 90m² or less? Would the lifestyle suit me? How many of us would be inhabiting this smaller space? Could we cull our belongings and store our sentimental memories inside ourselves, not on our shelves? Could we embrace the new technologies that make living with a lighter environmental footprint possible? Only you will be able to answer those questions, but if the answer is 'yes', here are some practical considerations.

/ Not every state is equal. Planning regulations vary from state to state and while some are very encouraging of the movement to live in smaller homes, others are not. Do your research and if yours is one of the states where intensification is still not the norm, then ask yourself if you're ready to move to one that is.

/ State by state legislation differs. So too does the way individual councils within the states interpret that legislation. Some allow two bedroom floorplans, some only one. Does this affect where you might decide to build your own small home?

/ Could you live in closer proximity with the neighbours? Privacy, noise, exterior lights: all of these are less controllable than they are in less dense housing situations. Would the benefits – proximity to the city, less maintenance – outweigh the possible downsides.

/ Getting the best out of a small block, maximising its use so that it suits your needs in every way, is likely to be a job for the experts. Embrace your architectural fraternity and go forward from there.

WHEN DESIGNING A SMALL HOUSE

Space

Rooms don't have to be big to work well. Well-planned smaller rooms are deceptively spacious. A well-designed small dwelling can offer the functionality of a much larger space – multifunctional use of space and multifunctional furnishings will eliminate the need for a large footprint. Utility areas can be well-planned vertical spaces, laundries tucked into the outside corner return of a run of cupboards, bedrooms uncluttered by built-in storage. Strategies like these allow the primary spaces to remain generous and interesting.

Volume

Height helps a small floorplan feel bigger. A generous ceiling height of 2.7m or more will enhance the impression of spaciousness. So too will voids, courtyards and strategically combining higher and lower ceilings.

Flow

Minimise the size of transitional spaces. Stairways, passages and entry areas are only used intermittently; reducing the space reserved for them leaves more for the living and bedrooms. Often these spaces appear bigger when the entry point to them has been constrained. Link rooms to external spaces as decks and courtyards can function as hallways and will visually extend the parameters of the room.

Light

Daylight, used in conjunction with volume and flow, is the cheapest way of enhancing the illusion of space. Bathrooms can be lit with skylights, living areas glazed where they connect to their outdoor living spaces. Sunlight also provides a passive heat source in cooler months (when used in conjunction with an exposed concrete slab) and yet can be controlled by the depth of eaves when too much of it is a good thing.

Orientation

North, south, east and west. All aspects have their qualities and all can be utilised when designing a small home from scratch. Your designer will consider how the orientation of a block can be optimised to fit a twenty-first century lifestyle – light, privacy, and use of indoor and outdoor spaces are all affected by orientation. Living spaces are best designed for the sun as this is where it will be most appreciated, utility spaces can be lit from above, bedrooms can be cooler and make best use of an easterly orientation.

A perimeter strategy

Urban infill sites are frequently overlooked, or in some way lacking in privacy. Local regulations will to some extent suggest how this is addressed, but considering options from the beginning of the design process will reap dividends.

Storage

Visual clutter is the enemy of living gracefully in a small space. Built-in storage allows every millimetre of the floorplan to be used to its best advantage. Remember that 600mm thick walls are storage units in their own right. Taking care with design will allow access from both sides while allowing a level of aural insulation impossible with a traditionally constructed single skin wall.

Technology

Embrace technology. Books and music can be stored and accessed electronically. Are you happy with this, or is the physical presence of belongings collected over a lifetime as important as what the object contains?

Furnishings

Large furnishings will not only look out of scale, they will also interfere with the way a room is used. Ensure every item is multifunctional, and that every element of an item justifies its inclusion – do sofas need big arms to be comfortable? Can a side table contain storage? Be prepared to have things custom-made to make the best use of your floorplan. The cost will be justified in the long term.

Design economically

Repetition of detail minimises costs as economies can be made in construction time, and utilising a standard grid (600mm modules) in the building materials you plan to use will reduce wastage.

DESIGN DIRECTORY

Architects, designers and builders whose work features in this book

A-CH (Atelier Chen Hung)
+61 (0)7 3846 3089
www.a-ch.com.au

ArchiBlox
+61 1300 773 122
www.archiblox.com.au

Archier
+61 (0) 424 956 318
www.archier.com.au

BAAhouse
+61 (0) 409 577 705
www.baahouse.com.au

Branch Studio Architects
+61 (0) 3 9419 2300
www.branchstudioarchitects.com

Day Bukh Architects
+61 (0) 400 661 788
www.daybukharchitects.com.au

Fred's Tiny Houses
www.fredstinyhouses.com.au
+61 (0) 408 330 420

Ben Giles Architect
+61 (0) 412 599 468
www.bengilesarchitect.com.au

Emma Hohnen
Self-Design and Owner
www.emmahohnen.com

Allison Hopper Architect
+61 (0) 417 240 822
ahopper@netspace.net.au

David Langston-Jones Architect
+61 (0) 2 9519 2919
www.davidlangston-jones.com.au

David Luck Architecture
+61 (0) 3 9867 7509
www.davidluckarchitecture.com.au

Misho + Associates
+61 (0) 3 6264 2333
www.misho.com.au

MODE Homes
+61 2 9029 0683
www.modehomes.com.au

Modscape
+61 3 9314 7769
www.modscape.com.au

REFRESH* DESIGN
+61 (0) 404 326 862
www.refreshdesign.com.au

Robeson Architects
+61 (0) 411 079 078
www.robesonarchitects.com.au

Room11
+61 (0) 3 6224 8642
www.room11.com.au

**Small Change Design
and Construction**
+61 (0) 3 9481 8725
www.smallchangedesign.com.au

Studio Edwards
+ 61 (0) 416 746 368
www.studio-edwards.com

Peter Stutchbury Architecture
+61 (2) 9979 5030
www.peterstutchbury.com.au

Takt | Studio for Architecture
+61 (0) 2 4268 4324
www.takt.net.au

David Weir Architects
+61(0) 8 9284 5499
www.davidweirarchitects.com

workbylizandalex
www.thebarntas.com

Acoustic glazing
Sometimes described as sound control glass, this is a high-tech laminated glass product with layers that reduce the ability of noise to travel between spaces - either from exterior to interior - or between specialised internal spaces such as a sound studio.

Bargeboards
A timber board, typically decorative, which is in some way fixed to the gable end of a roof to hide the ends of the roof timbers and to prevent water entering the roof cavity.

Cladding
Internal or internal wall coverings.

Energy rating
This is the efficiency of a structure or appliance measured in terms of its annual energy (electricity, gas etc) consumption. In Australia, both houses and appliances have a star rating system; the more stars the more economical the item is to run.

FCB
Fibre Cement Board or concrete board. This is a low-cost wall cladding whose weathertightness relies on a cavity wall design, correct flashings and a meticulous attention to the sealing of all joints. Formply A resin-impregnated board with a smooth, slightly glossy, black surface. Although increasingly popular as interior cladding, its traditional use in the construction industry is as a material for formwork in the manufacture of concrete pre-formed panels.

Gable roof
Commonly called a pitched roof, a gable roof has triangular portions at each end - these are the gables - and a ridge line connecting the apex of each triangle. Sloping planes fall away from the ridge line and are contained, and to some extent supported, at each end of the structure by the gable.

High and low thermal mass
Thermal mass is the ability of a material to absorb and store heat and energy. Heavy weight materials, such as brick and concrete require a lot of heat to change temperature, and as such are described as having a high thermal mass. Lightweight materials such as timber have low thermal mass.

Hip roof
A hip roof is the type of roof where all sides slope downwards at an angle from an apex towards the walls. In its simplest form, it has four sloping planes and no gables or other vertical areas. More typically it is combined with a gable roof to produce the typical suburban bungalow roofline.

Jointers
External jointers are timber or aluminium mouldings which cover the joins between sheet material claddings. Used in 'biscuit' form they allow (in conjunction with glue) an invisible joint between timber edges, for example in a timber worktop.

Low-e glazing
High tech glazing with properties that modify the amount of heat able to enter the interior of a building.

Macrocarpa
A hardy durable wood that weathers to a silver finish without any treatment.

Shiplap
Pre-formed boards fitted together by halving so that each one overlaps the one below. It is a

particularly weathertight type of cladding that originated in the shipping industry as cladding for wooden ships. Traditional weatherboarding creates weathertightness by overlapping the board below, but without the pre-formed profile.

Shoji screen
Originating in Japan, a shoji screen is a sliding door made from a rice-paper-covered timber lattice. In contemporary structures, the rice paper is commonly replaced with a lookalike fibreglass product or glass.

Skillion roof
A steeply sloping, mono-pitched roof, frequently, although not always, with a line of high-level glazing under the higher edge. They are commonly called 'shed roofs' in Australia.

Soffits
The trimmed underside of an architectural structure such as the eaves of a house, an archway or a balcony. In Australian usage, this is most commonly the horizontal area between the vertical wall and the edge of the roof, and is clad in various ways to assist weathertightness and to add decorative interest.

Solar gain
The increase in temperature in a space or structure that results from solar radiation. In architectural usage 'solar heat gain' or 'passive solar gain' is where a structure is designed so that the orientation of the structure and the materials used allows the building to semi-warm itself without mechanical assistance – most frequently by use of a north-facing exposed concrete slab. Deep eaves assist in the control of overheating in the warmer months when the sun is higher.

Stud height
The height of a ceiling

Tongue and groove
Wooden planking in which adjacent boards are joined by means of interlocking ridges and hollows down their sides. It is frequently used on a vertical exterior with rough sawn timber in a semi-rustic style. It used to be a common way of making a hardwood floor but it's an expensive option as it requires using solid timber and has now largely been replaced with engineered timber overlay flooring.

Tsubo
A traditional Japanese unit of measurement equal to approximately 3.31m². Two commonly-sized tatami mats are equal to one *tsubo*. Post-war social housing in Japan was frequently constructed using a nine *tsubo* grid.

Zincalume
This is a commonly used tradenamed product for metal cladding made from rolled steel which is coated with an alloy composed of 55% aluminium, 43.5% zinc and 1.5% silicon. The combination provides a superior coating, both on the cut edges and on the flat surface, resulting in an overall superior corrosion performance. It can be found either in corrugated or flat form.

REFERENCES

Books

Benitez, Cristina, *Small Eco Houses: Living Green in Style*, Universe, New York 2010

Conran, Terence, *How to Live in Small Places*, Conran Octopus, London, 2006

Crafti, Stephen, *Affordable Architecture: Great Houses on a Budget*, Images Publishing Group, Mulgrave, VIC., 2010

Ehmann, S and Borges, S (eds), *Rock the Shack: The Architecture of Cabins, Cocoons and Hide-Outs*, Gestalten, Berlin, 2013

Foster, Catherine, *Small House Living: Design Conscious New Zealand Homes of 90m² or Less*. Penguin Books, Auckland, 2015

Harrison, Stuart, *46 Square Metres of Land Doesn't Normally Become a House,* Thames and Hudson, Melbourne, 2011

Jodidio, Philip, *Small Architecture Now!* Taschen, New York, 2014

Kahn, Lloyd, *Tiny Homes, Simple Shelter,* Shelter Publications, Bolinas, CA, 2012

Koones, Sheri, *Prefabulous World: Energy-Efficient and Sustainable Homes Around the Globe*, Harry N. Abrams, New York, 2014

McCall, Claire, *Green Modern*, Penguin, Auckland, 2014

Mora, Francesc Zamora, *New Small Spaces: Good Ideas*, Collins Design, New York, 2008

Richardson, Phyllis, *XS: Big Ideas, Small Buildings*, Thames & Hudson, London, 2001

Richardson, Phyllis, *Nano House: Innovations for Small Dwellings*, Thames & Hudson, London, 2011

Richardson, Phyllis, *Superlight: Lightness in Contemporary Houses,* Thames & Hudson, London, 2014

Roke, Rebecca, *Nanotecture: Tiny Built Things*, Phaidon, London, 2016

Walsh, John and Reynolds, Patrick, *Big House Small House*, Godwit, Auckland, 2012

Zeiger, Mimi, *Tiny Houses*, Rizzoli, New York, 2009

Magazines

Home NZ: Special Issue. *Small Houses: Eight little New Zealand homes that think big*, Bauer Media Group, Auckland, Aug/Sept 2016

Online

architetcetera.blogspot.co.nz

archinspire.pro/46sqm-small-house-plan-basic-need-self-sufficient-project

houzz.com.au

lifeedited.com

remodelista.com/get-inspired/architecture-interiors

smallhouseswoon.com

smallhousebliss.com

INDEX

ACKNOWLEDGEMENTS

No book like this would be possible without the co-operation and support of the owners, and the professionalism and creativity of the architects and designers they commissioned to bring their visions of small, perfect spaces to life. Also essential is the photographers' magical third eye. Without it, the experience of 'walking' through these homes would be much the poorer. Thank you all so much.

Thanks also for the stern first edit from Luke Dixon, my in-house editor, and to my publisher, Katrina O'Brien, and the team at Penguin Random House. Together they have enabled my love of small-project architecture to be shared with the wider world. To all of them I owe my heartfelt thanks.

But without the love and encouragement of my children – Daniel, Corrina and Luke – nothing would be possible at all. May they all one day have a small house to call their own.

VIKING

UK | USA | Canada | Ireland
Australia | India | New Zealand
South Africa | China

Penguin Books is part of the Penguin Random House group
of companies whose addresses can be found at
global.penguinrandomhouse.com.

First published by Penguin Random House Australia Pty Ltd, 2017.

Design by Emily O'Neill © Penguin Random House Australia Pty Ltd

Photographer for each house credited on chapter opener;
additional photos by Daniel Dixon (cover), Alicia Taylor (pages 1, 239),
Dion Robeson (pages 2-3, 6), Shantanu Starick (pages 4-5),
Michael Nicholson (page 240).

Printed and bound in China by
RR Donnelley Asia Printing Solutions Ltd

National Library of Australia
Cataloguing-in-Publication data:

Foster, Catherine, author.
Small House Living Australia / Catherine Foster
9780143783619 (paperback)

Subjects: Architecture, Domestic--Environmental aspects--Australia.
Small houses--Australia.
Sustainable architecture--Australia.
Sustainable living--Australia.
Dwellings--Australia.

penguin.com.au